TELL ME ABOUT
THE NATURAL WORLD

An Hachette UK Company
www.hachette.co.uk

First published in Great Britain in 2016 by Chancellor Press,
a division of Octopus Publishing Group Ltd
Carmelite House, 50 Victoria Embankment, London EC4Y 0DZ
www.octopusbooks.co.uk

Edited and designed by Anna Southgate and Leah Germann

ISBN 978-0-7537-3031-7

A CIP catalogue record for this book is available from the British Library

Printed and bound in China

10 9 8 7 6 5 4 3 2 1

Publisher: Lucy Pessell
Design Manager: Megan van Staden
Editor: Natalie Bradley
Production Controller: Sarah Kulasek-Boyd

UPDATED & REVISED

TELL ME ABOUT
THE NATURAL WORLD

ANSWERS TO HUNDREDS OF
FASCINATING QUESTIONS

CHANCELLOR
PRESS

CONTENTS

OUR
PLANET

CONTENTS

WHERE IS THE EARTH'S MANTLE?

Beneath the Earth's crust is a sphere of hot rock and metal. By studying the records of earthquake waves, scientists have learned that the inside of the Earth is divided into three parts: the mantle, the outer core and the inner core.

The mantle is a thick layer of rock below the crust. It goes down about 2,900km (1,800 miles). The rock in the mantle is made of silicon, oxygen, aluminium, iron and magnesium. The uppermost part of the mantle has a temperature of about 870°C (1600°F). The temperature gradually increases to about 4400°C (8000°F) in the deepest part of the mantle. The outer core begins about 2,900km (1,800 miles) below the Earth's surface. The ball-shaped inner core lies within the outer core and makes up the middle of the Earth.

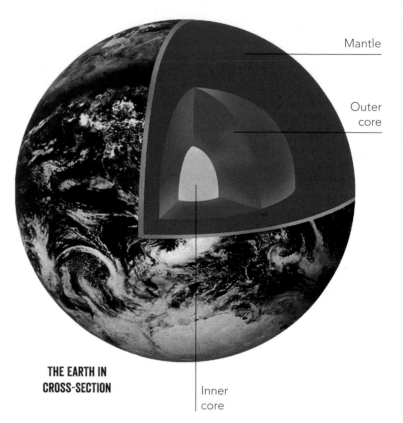

Mantle

Outer core

Inner core

THE EARTH IN CROSS-SECTION

FACT FILE

The inner core rotates more rapidly than the remainder of the planet. During a period of about 400 years, the inner core rotates around the Earth's axis one more time than the surface does.

Sometimes, bits of rock from Earth's mantle come to the surface in volcanic eruptions.

WHERE IS
THE HYDROSPHERE?

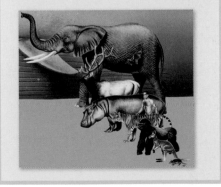

Earth's hydrosphere

All bodies of water and ice – as well as water in the atmosphere – make up the Earth's hydrosphere. The Earth's surface is 71 per cent water – almost all of it in the oceans. The waters of the hydrosphere are important in many ways. Animals and plants need water to live. Plants use water to make food, and are eaten by human beings and animals. Water also wears away rocks and slowly turns them into soil that is necessary for growing crops. Oceans and other large bodies of water also help control the Earth's weather and climate. The temperature of water does not change as fast as that of land. Wind blowing over a large body of water can keep land from becoming extremely hot or extremely cold.

DID YOU KNOW THAT WATER EXISTS IN THREE MAIN STATES ON EARTH? IT CAN BE A LIQUID, A GAS (STEAM) OR A SOLID (ICE)?

• FACT FILE •

All the Earth's animals and plants live on the Earth's surface or close to the surface – underground, underwater or in the atmosphere. The region where life is found is called the Earth's biosphere.

WHAT IS THE LARGEST OCEAN?

The Pacific Ocean, the largest and deepest of the world's four oceans, covers more than one-third of the Earth's surface and contains more than half of its free water. It is sometimes divided into two nominal sections: the part north of the equator is called the North Pacific; the part south of the equator, the South Pacific. It is bounded on the east by the North and South American continents; on the north by the Bering Strait; on the west by Asia, the Malay Archipelago and Australia; and on the south by Antarctica.

The name 'Pacific', which means peaceful, was given to it by the Portuguese navigator Ferdinand Magellan in 1520. The Pacific is the oldest of the existing ocean basins, its oldest rocks having been dated at 200 million years.

360 million sq km (140 million sq miles) of Earth's surface is covered by water.

Earth's main oceans are the Pacific, the Atlantic, the Arctic, the Indian and the Southern.

WHAT IS A SAVANNA?

African savanna

A savanna, also spelled savannah, is a grassland with widely scattered trees and shrubs. Most savannas are in the tropics and lie between deserts and rainforests. Savannas cover more than two-fifths of Africa and large areas of Australia, India and South America. They occur in regions that have both rainy and dry seasons. The growth of trees on savannas is limited by the dry season, which may last up to five months. When the dry season begins, grasses stop growing and turn brown, and most trees shed their leaves. Only the most drought-resistant trees can survive. Most savanna grasses grow in clumps. Acacias, baobabs and palms are some of the more common savanna trees.

THE DRY SEASON ON THE SAVANNA IS REALLY DRY WITH ONLY ABOUT 10CM (4IN) OF RAIN FROM OCTOBER TO MARCH!

WHAT SHAPES THE SEA FLOOR?

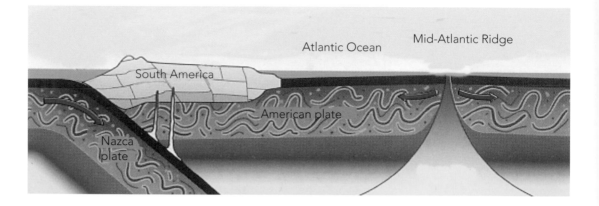

South America

Atlantic Ocean

Mid-Atlantic Ridge

American plate

Nazca plate

The bottom of the ocean has features as varied as those on land. Huge plains spread out across the ocean floor, and long mountain chains rise towards the surface. Volcanoes erupt from the ocean bottom, and deep valleys cut through the floor. In the early 1960s, a theory called sea-floor spreading provided some explanation. According to the theory, the sea floor itself moves, carrying the continents along. Circulating movements deep within the Earth's mantle make the sea floor move. The circulating movements carry melted rock up to the mid-ocean ridges and force it into the central valleys of the ridges. As the melted rock cools and hardens, it forms new sea floor and pushes the old floor and the continents away from the ridges.

FACT FILE

A hot vent is a chimney-like structure on the ocean floor that discharges hot, mineral-rich water. Scientists first observed hot vents in 1977, in the Galapagos Rift, a region on the floor of the Pacific Ocean.

 THE DEEPEST POINT IN THE WORLD'S SEA FLOOR IS CALLED CHALLENGER DEEP. IT HAS A DEPTH OF ALMOST 11,000M (36,000FT)!

WHAT ARE CONTINENTAL SHELVES?

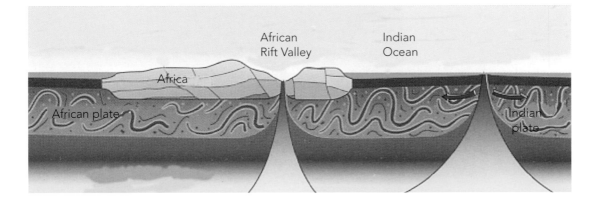

African Rift Valley

Indian Ocean

Africa

African plate

Indian plate

The continental margin forms the part of the seabed that borders the continents. It consists of the continental shelf, the continental slope and the continental rise. The continental shelf is the submerged land at the edge of the continents. It begins at the shoreline and gently slopes underwater to an average depth of about 130m (430ft). The width of the continental shelf averages 75km (47 miles). In certain areas, such as parts of the Arctic region, the shelf extends as far as 1,600km (1,000 miles). In some other areas, particularly those bordering much of the Pacific, it measures only 1.6km (1 mile) or less. Valleys of varying depths cut through the shelf.

Earth's seven continents are Africa, Antarctica, Asia, Australia, Europe, North America and South America.

• FACT FILE •

The continental rise consists of sediment from the continental shelf that accumulates at the bottom of the slope. These deposits can extend up to about 1,000km (600 miles) from the slope.

HOW DOES LIFE EXIST IN THE ARCTIC?

The Arctic is not continuously covered in snow and ice – in the south the marshy tundra can support herds of thousands of reindeer (caribou) in the summer.

In winter, however, conditions are far harsher, and the biting wind is the main problem. Animals have various ways of coping. Some, like reindeer, Arctic terns and snow geese avoid it by migrating south. Some larger mammals, such as polar bears and Arctic foxes have thick coats and develop a dense layer of insulating body fat in autumn to keep the winter wind out. Arctic hares, lemmings and other small mammals burrow under the snow in the worst weather. Surprisingly, very few mammals hibernate.

An Arctic fox

FACT FILE

There are about 40,000 polar bears living in the Arctic regions, but their numbers are dwindling owing to scarce food resources.

THE LOWEST TEMPERATURE EVER RECORDED IN THE ARCTIC IS −68°C (−90.4°F). IT WAS MEASURED IN SIBERIA.

WHAT
SHAPES THE COASTS?

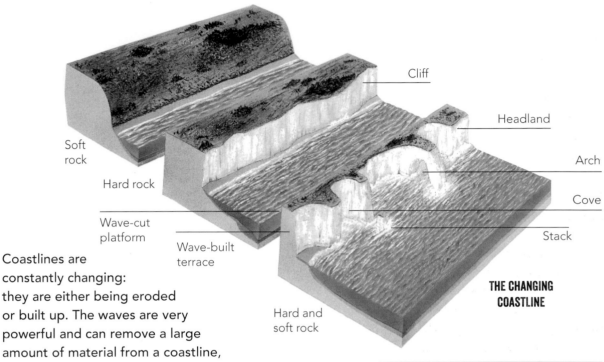

Cliff

Headland

Arch

Cove

Stack

Soft rock

Hard rock

Wave-cut platform

Wave-built terrace

Hard and soft rock

THE CHANGING COASTLINE

Coastlines are constantly changing: they are either being eroded or built up. The waves are very powerful and can remove a large amount of material from a coastline, especially during a storm. The sand and pebbles removed from the coastline are carried by the sea and can be dropped further along a coast or out at sea.

Many coastal features can be made by the steady erosion of the cliffs and headlands such as sand dunes, spits and salt marshes. A beach can make the waves less powerful and reduce the amount of erosion of the coast. Steep cliffs and wave-cut platforms can be formed in areas of hard rock. A bay can be carved out in an area where hard rock has soft rock between it.

DID YOU KNOW THAT THERE ARE AROUND 620,000KM (372,000 MILES) OF COASTLINE IN THE WORLD?

• FACT FILE •

Many cliffs on the coast are made up of chalk. Chalk is formed from the skeletons of millions and millions of tiny animals called *foraminifera*. It is a sedimentary rock that formed millions of years ago beneath shallow seas.

WHAT CAUSES TIDES?

Earth | Moon |

The daily rise and fall of the ocean's tides occurs because of the pull of gravity of the Moon. As the Earth spins round, the water in the oceans is 'pulled' towards the Moon slightly, making a bulge. There is a corresponding bulge on the other side of the Earth. Wherever the bulges are positioned it is high tide. In between, the water is shallower and so it is low tide. High tides occur every 25 hours, because at the same time that the Earth is spinning on its axis, the Moon is travelling around the Earth once every 27 days. So high tides are about one hour later every day.

DID YOU KNOW THAT SOME PLACES HAVE TWO HIGH AND TWO LOW TIDES A DAY, WHILE OTHERS HAVE ONLY ONE HIGH AND ONE LOW TIDE IN A DAY?

• FACT FILE •

Spring tides are tides with unusually high ranges that occur twice per month when the Sun, Earth and Moon are in line. They can be especially high in the spring and autumn.

WHAT ARE CURRENTS?

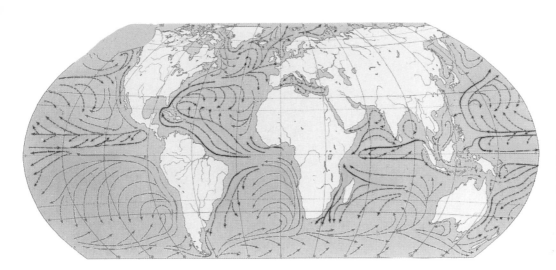

OCEAN CURRENTS

Summer in the northern hemisphere: cold currents are shown in blue, warm in red.

A rip current is a strong narrow current of water that sometimes occurs where there are breaking waves on beaches. The current runs against the flow of the waves and can be dangerous for swimmers.

The ocean waters are moved by the wind on their surface and by movements within the ocean. These currents are able to transfer a great amount of heat around the Earth as they move and thus play a part in climate control. The spinning of the Earth dictates the way the water circulates. In the northern hemisphere it moves clockwise and in the southern hemisphere, anti-clockwise. Ocean currents vary in the summer and winter and a change in wind direction can change the current, influencing the weather in a particular country. A cold ocean current makes the weather colder and a warm one, warmer.

• FACT FILE •

A whirlpool is a mass of water that spins around and around in one direction and with great force. It may occur when opposing currents of water meet, or it may be caused by the action of the wind.

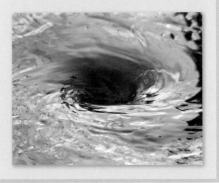

WHEN DO RIVERS BEGIN?

There are two main ways in which rivers begin. Some rivers start when a natural spring releases water from underground. These are often small trickles of water, which develop into little streams. In turn these streams increase in size until they are acknowledged as rivers. Other rivers begin when persistent rain makes a groove or a channel in a piece of land. As more and more rain falls into this channel, a flow of water slowly begins. Just like the springs, a stream can soon develop into a river.

• FACT FILE •

When rivers reach land close to sea level, they begin to meander, forming a snake-like shape on the land. This is caused by the gradual dropping of the sediment it carries where the flow is weak.

DID YOU KNOW THAT THE NILE IS THE WORLD'S LONGEST RIVER? IT TRAVELS A WHOPPING 6,650KM (4,132 MILES) THROUGH ELEVEN COUNTRIES, INCLUDING KENYA, UGANDA, CONGO, RWANDA, ETHIOPIA AND EGYPT.

WHAT SHAPES A RIVER?

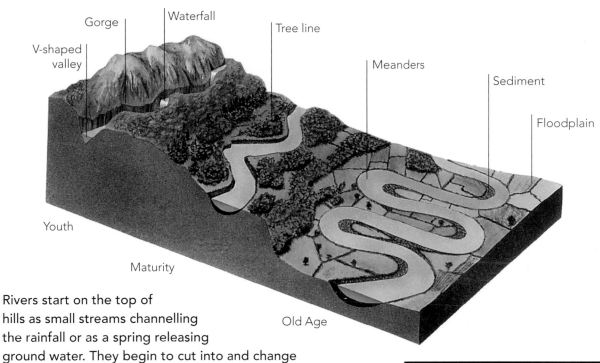

V-shaped valley

Gorge

Waterfall

Tree line

Meanders

Sediment

Floodplain

Youth

Maturity

Old Age

Rivers start on the top of hills as small streams channelling the rainfall or as a spring releasing ground water. They begin to cut into and change the landscape on the way to the sea. In the highlands the water can move very quickly and has a lot of power. The river can cut deep gorges and V-shaped valleys in the softer rocks. In the harder rocks they can form waterfalls. The river moves rocks and pebbles along its bed by bouncing and rolling. The lighter sediments are carried or dissolved in the water. When the river reaches the more gentle slopes, it becomes wider and moves more slowly. Mud and sand is dropped when the river floods and forms ridges along the river bank. When the river reaches the lower plains it begins to meander.

The loops and bends that you see in river valleys are called meanders. They happen when one side of the river erodes its banks more, because the water there is travelling faster.

• FACT FILE •

The further a river is from its source on a mountainside, the slower the water travels. This is because the river eventually reaches flatter ground and widens before it reaches the sea.

WHERE IS THE SNOW LINE?

Earth has several great mountain ranges, among them the Alps, the Rockies, the Himalayas, the Andes and the Atlas Mountains.

The snow line is the lower limit of the area on a mountain where snow is present all year. It is not at the same height everywhere: in Africa it is far higher than it is in the Alps of Europe or the Rocky Mountains in North America, because the surrounding lands are hotter. In any location, it is not even the same from year to year as more snow will melt in hotter summers. In many parts of the world, the snow line is, like glaciers, retreating up the mountains as climate change seems to be causing longer, hotter summers and shorter winters with less snowfall.

• FACT FILE •

Artificial snow is produced at some ski resorts. It is made from partly frozen droplets of water. Machines make this 'snow' by spraying a mixture of freezing water into the air.

WHERE IS THE ALPINE SLOPE?

?

DID YOU KNOW THAT THE ALPS CONTAIN AROUND 100 PEAKS THAT ARE HIGHER THAN 4,000M (13,000FT)? THEY ARE KNOWN AS THE 'FOUR-THOUSANDERS'.

The Alpine Slope is part of the Alps, a mountain range in south-central Europe. The landscape includes huge mountains and deep valleys with forests of beech, oak and chestnut trees growing on the lower slopes of the mountains. At higher levels there are grasslands and pine forests. Only low bushes grow at still higher elevations, while the mountaintops are covered in rocks and glaciers. Melting snow from the Alps feeds many rivers. Hydroelectric plants along Alpine rivers provide much of Italy's electric power. The people of the Alpine region live in small, scattered communities, and make their living by farming and herding. Many tourists visit the Alps to ski.

• FACT FILE •

The Apennines stretch almost the entire length of Italy. These mountains have steep inclines of soft rock that are constantly being eroded as a result of heavy rains, overgrazing of sheep and goats, and the clearing of forests for timber and farmland.

WHERE WOULD YOU SEE A STALACTITE?

Stalactites are seen in limestone caverns. They are icicle-shaped masses of calcite attached to the roof of the cave. Stalactites are mineral deposits that form in caves, sometimes collectively called dripstone. Ground water trickling through cracks in the roofs of such caverns contains dissolved calcium bicarbonate. When a drop of water comes into contact with the air of the cavern, some of the calcium bicarbonate is transformed into calcium carbonate which forms a ring of calcite on the roof of the cavern. As this process is repeated time and time again, the length and thickness of the stalactite is increased.

FACT FILE

A stalagmite is a cone of mineral deposit that rises from the floor of a cave. A useful way of remembering the difference between stalactites and stalagmites is to say: stalactites hang 'tite' to the ceiling while stalagmites hold with all their 'mite' to the floor!

ONE OF THE LONGEST STALACTITES IN THE WORLD CAN BE FOUND IN A LIMESTONE CAVE CALLED POL AN IONIAN IN COUNTY CLARE, IRELAND. IT IS AROUND 7M (24FT) LONG.

WHERE DO
TROPICAL RAINFORESTS GROW?

Tropical rainforests grow near the Equator, in regions where it is hot and wet almost all year round. The biggest areas are in the Amazon Basin of South America and the Congo Basin in West Africa. The forest canopy at the treetops is very dense, so not much light reaches the forest floor, except in clearings where old trees have fallen, which are rapidly colonized by small plants. Rainforests are important because they have a wide diversity of plants and animals. They also absorb large amounts of carbon dioxide, one of the major greenhouse gases, and so help to slow down the greenhouse effect.

?

DID YOU KNOW THAT RAINFORESTS ARE HOME TO MORE THAN 2,000 SPECIES OF ANIMALS? THEY INCLUDE BOA CONSTRICTORS, GIANT ANTEATERS, JAGUARS, MARMOSETS AND POISON DART FROGS.

WHERE IS THE
GREAT SALT LAKE DESERT?

The Great Salt Lake Desert is west of Salt Lake City in Utah in the Western United States. Mineral-rich waters are brought to the lake and then evaporate (there is no outlet to the sea), leaving the minerals behind. Great Salt Lake and other smaller lakes in the area are the remnants of Lake Bonneville, which was far bigger, but also had no outlet to the sea for most of its history. The desert is the salt layers deposited by this lake's evaporation. Like the Dead Sea, the waters in some parts of the lake are saline enough for people to float on, but unlike the Dead Sea, the Great Salt Lake is visited by large colonies of wading birds. The level of the waters in the lake can fluctuate rapidly: at one time it was so high that water had to be pumped out, while in recent years, lack of rainfall has caused the lake to shrink.

WHERE IS THE WORLD'S LARGEST HOT DESERT?

The world's largest hot desert is the Sahara in northern Africa. It stretches from the Atlantic Ocean in the west to the Red Sea in the east. As well as the sand dunes that people associate with deserts, it also has high, rocky plateaux, mountains and areas of semi-desert. The only water apart from minimal seasonal rainfall is found in oases and in the River Nile. Today, people live around the edge of the desert and some live at or travel between the oases, but thousands of years ago when it was wetter, people also lived in the desert's interior and many of their cave and rock paintings – called petroglyphs – have been found.

Because a desert is defined by the amount of rainfall or snowfall it receives, the largest desert in the world is, in fact, the icy continent of Antarctica.

WHEN ARE VOLCANOES DORMANT?

DIFFERENT TYPES OF VOLCANIC ERUPTION

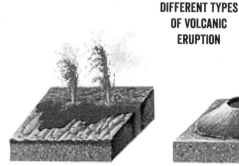

Fissure eruptions release runny lava.

In Hawaiian eruptions the lava is less fluid and produces low cones.

Volcanic eruptions are more violent and eject solid lava.

The word dormant actually means 'sleeping'. So when people talk about a volcano being dormant, it really means it is temporarily sleeping and might erupt at any time in the future. An extinct volcano, on the other hand, is one that will not become active again.

Like earthquakes, volcanoes mainly occur along fault lines. Molten rock, gases and ash are forced out through a gap in the Earth's crust to release the pressure that has built up. When there is very little pressure the volcano can remain in a dormant state for many many years. On the island of Maui there is a volcano called Haleakala which rises to a height of about 3,057 m (10,025 ft). It is the world's largest inactive volcano. Its crater is about 32 km (20 miles) around and some 829 m (2,720 ft deep).

WHEN WAS THE WORST VOLCANIC ERUPTION?

Strombolian eruptions blow out incandescent material.

In the Peléean type, a blocked vent is cleared explosively.

A Plinian eruption is a continuous blast of gas that rises to immense heights.

The island of Krakatau, Indonesia (west of Java) was a small volcanic island. The volcano itself had laid dormant for over 200 years until August 1883. On 20 May one of the cones erupted violently and three months later the whole island blew up. It was the biggest explosion in recorded history. For two and a half days the island was in total darkness because of the amount of dust in the air. A cloud of ash rose 80km (50 miles) into the air. The eruption caused a tidal wave, killing 36,000 people.

THE KRAKATAU EXPLOSION COULD BE HEARD AND FELT IN AUSTRALIA, 3,500KM (2,000 MILES) AWAY.

• FACT FILE •

On 24 August in the year 79 CE, there was a great eruption of Mount Vesuvius, a volcano in southern Italy. The lava, stones and ashes thrown up by the volcano completely buried two nearby towns.

WHERE IS SEDIMENTARY ROCK FOUND?

Sedimentary rocks develop from materials that once were part of older rocks or of plants or animals. These materials were worn away from the land. They then collected in low places, layer upon layer, and hardened into rock. Many sedimentary rocks contain shells, bones and other remains of living things. Such remains, or the impressions of remains in sedimentary rocks, are called fossils. Metamorphic rocks are formed deep in the crust when igneous and sedimentary rocks are changed by heat and the weight of the Earth's crust presses on them. Igneous rocks are formed when melted rock deep inside the Earth's crust cools and hardens – or erupts at the surface as lava.

Sedimentary rock is found in the Earth's crust along with two other kinds of rock: igneous and metamorphic.

WHAT CAUSES LAND EROSION?

Erosion is a natural process by which rock and soil are broken loose from the Earth's surface at one location and moved to another. Erosion changes land by wearing down mountains, filling in valleys and making rivers appear and disappear. It is usually a slow and gradual process that occurs over thousands or millions of years.

Erosion begins with a process called weathering. In this process, environmental factors break rock and soil into smaller pieces and loosen them from the Earth's surface. A chief cause is the formation of ice. As water freezes, it expands with great force. As a result, when it freezes inside the crack of a rock, it can break the rock apart.

Rivers can be a cause of erosion. They carry small bits of rock that scrape away at the river banks as they flow downstream.

• FACT FILE •

Erosion can be speeded up by such human activities such as farming and mining. One of the most harmful effects of erosion is that it robs farmland of productive topsoil.

WHAT ERODES THE DESERTS?

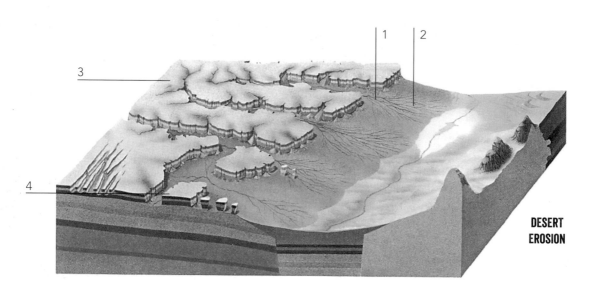

DESERT EROSION

A desert landscape includes various kinds of surface features created by water and wind erosion and by deposits of silt, sand and other sediments. The drainage system is made up of normally dry streams called arroyos. After a rainfall, water fills the stream channels called wadi (1). The rapidly flowing water cuts away the rocks of desert mountains and carries sediments to the mouth of mountain canyons. There, deposits of sediments create fan-shaped forms known as alluvial fans (2). Sometimes, the streams carry water into low areas in the desert plains and form temporary lakes. The water that collects in these lakes either evaporates or seeps into the ground. Water erosion also creates big flat-topped hills known as mesas (3) and smaller flat-topped hills called buttes (4).

• FACT FILE •

Vast regions covered by sand and dunes are called sand seas. Sand seas cover large areas in desert regions of Africa, Asia and Australia.

WHERE ARE THE SEVEN NATURAL WONDERS OF THE WORLD?

Although there is no official list, the following are generally accepted as the Seven Natural Wonders of the World. In the United States Meteor Crater, also known as Barringer Crater, is a huge circular depression in the Earth near Winslow, Arizona, caused by a meteorite impact and the Grand Canyon is a breathtaking 450-km (280-mile) chasm created by the Colorado River eroding the rock of the Colorado plateau over about 6 million years. Asia's Mount Everest, rising 8,850m (29,035ft) above sea level in the Himalayas, is the world's highest mountain. In central Australia Uluru (Ayers Rock) rises 346m (1,141ft) above the desert floor and off the east coast the Great Barrier Reef is the world's longest coral reef formation at about 2,010km (1,250 miles) in length. Europe's

The Matterhorn

Matterhorn, on the Italian-Swiss border, is one of the most beautiful mountains on Earth and in southern Africa, the spectacular Victoria Falls is on the Zambezi between Zimbabwe and Zambia.

FACT FILE

Uluru (Ayers Rock) is loaf-shaped and has a circumference of about 9km (5½ miles). It is composed of red sandstone. It is a sacred site for the local Native Australians.

CLIMATE AND ENVIRONMENT

CONTENTS

WHAT IS CLIMATE?

Sub-polar and temperate climate zones

Dry and subtropical climate zones

Tropical climate zones

Temporate climate zones

Climate is the word we use to describe the seasonal pattern of hot and cold, wet and dry weather, averaged over 30 years. There are four types of climate: these are tropical (hot and wet), desert (dry), temperate (mild), and polar (cold). As different parts of the Earth are closer to the Sun for longer, the climate varies in different countries. Those nearest the Equator are the hottest. Those nearest the poles are the coldest. Winds and ocean currents distribute the heat around the Earth. The weather pattern in different regions will also be altered by the changing seasons and some areas routinely have a higher level of annual rainfall than others, while some countries remain very dry.

In recent decades, environmentalists have shown that global warming might contribute to climate change.

• FACT FILE •

Mountains, such as the Rockies in North America, have a typical alpine climate because of their height above sea level.

HOW DOES PRESSURE AFFECT OUR WEATHER?

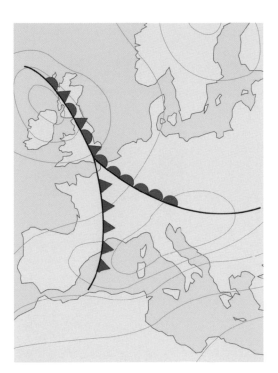

Weather is simply what the air or atmosphere is like at that time. No matter what the air is – cold, cool, warm, hot, calm, breezy, windy, dry, moist or wet – that is still weather. Air pressure differs across all parts of the Earth's surface, and this difference causes winds. Air will move from an area of high pressure, or an anticyclone, to an area of low pressure, or a depression. Depressions are usually associated with bad weather conditions and rain. These changes in air pressure can be measured by an instrument called a barometer.

When meteorologists talk about a weather front, they are referring to the boundary between two masses of air at different temperatures and pressures. Increasingly accurate forecasting is now possible with the aid of satellites in space and computer technology.

FACT FILE

A lightning strike discharges about 100 million volts of electricity and heats the air in its path to more than 33,000°C (59,432°F). It can strike at an incredible 299,792km (186,300 miles) per second.

?

DID YOU KNOW THAT WEATHER SATELLITES MONITOR MORE THAN THE WEATHER? THEY CAN ALSO SPOT LARGE FIRES, SAND STORMS, DUST STORMS, POLLUTION, SNOW COVER AND MORE.

WHAT IS THE WATER CYCLE?

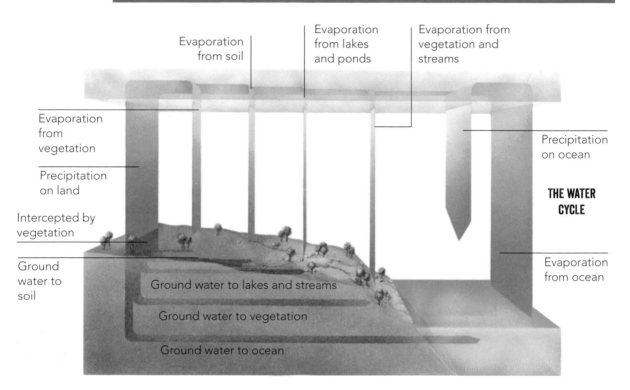

Evaporation from soil

Evaporation from lakes and ponds

Evaporation from vegetation and streams

Evaporation from vegetation

Precipitation on land

Intercepted by vegetation

Ground water to soil

Precipitation on ocean

THE WATER CYCLE

Evaporation from ocean

Ground water to lakes and streams

Ground water to vegetation

Ground water to ocean

Hydrology is the study of the movement and distribution of the waters of the Earth. People use billions of gallons of fresh water every day. In nature, water circulates through a system called the water cycle or hydrologic cycle. This cycle begins when heat from the Sun causes ocean water to evaporate. The vaporized water in the atmosphere gradually cools and forms clouds. The water eventually falls as rain or snow. Most rain and snow falls back into the oceans. But some falls on the land and flows back to the seas, completing the cycle.

There is much more fresh water in the ground than there is in the world's lakes and rivers?

• FACT FILE •

There are two main sources of fresh water: surface water and groundwater. Surface water flows over the land in lakes, rivers and streams. Groundwater seeps through the soil or through tiny cracks in rock.

WHAT IS THE WATER TABLE?

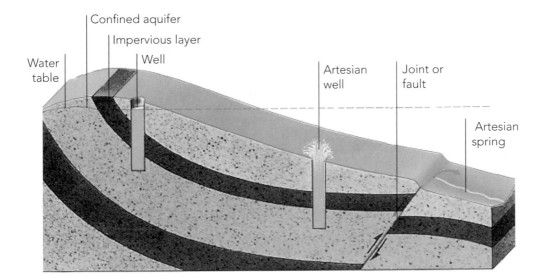

Confined aquifer
Impervious layer
Well
Water table
Artesian well
Joint or fault
Artesian spring

Groundwater is water beneath the surface of the Earth. It is the source of water for wells and many springs. Groundwater accumulates chiefly from rain and melted snow that filters through the soil. It also collects from water that seeps into the ground from lakes and ponds. The water settles into the pores and cracks of underground rocks and into the spaces between grains of sand and pieces of gravel.

A layer or bed of such porous material that yields useful amounts of groundwater is called an aquifer. Wells are drilled down to aquifers to draw groundwater to the surface.

The level of groundwater, called the water table, drops when more water is withdrawn than can be replaced naturally. Many regions of the world are using up the groundwater faster than aquifers are being replenished.

• FACT FILE •

Pollution of groundwater is a serious problem, especially near cities and industrial sites. Pollutants that seep into the ground result from contaminated surface water, leaks from sewage pipes and septic tanks, and chemical spills

WHAT IS PRECIPITATION?

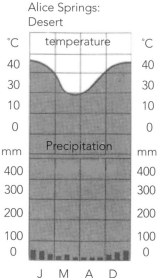

Alice Springs:
Desert

°C — temperature
- 40
- 30
- 10
- 0

mm — Precipitation
- 400
- 300
- 200
- 100
- 0

J M A D

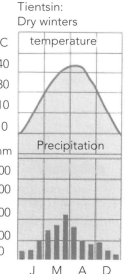

Tientsin:
Dry winters

°C — temperature
- 40
- 30
- 10
- 0

mm — Precipitation
- 400
- 300
- 200
- 100
- 0

J M A D

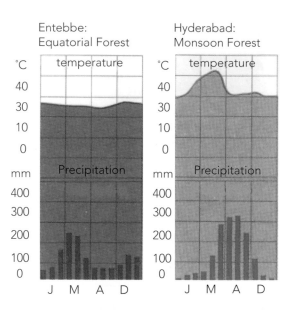

Entebbe:
Equatorial Forest

°C — temperature
- 40
- 30
- 10
- 0

mm — Precipitation
- 400
- 300
- 200
- 100
- 0

J M A D

Hyderabad:
Monsoon Forest

°C — temperature
- 40
- 30
- 10
- 0

mm — Precipitation
- 400
- 300
- 200
- 100
- 0

J M A D

MAWSYNRAM IN THE STATE OF MEGHALAYA, INDIA HAS NEARLY 12,000MM (470IN) OF RAIN A YEAR! IT IS THE WETTEST PLACE ON EARTH.

Rain falls throughout most of the world. In the tropics, almost all precipitation is rain. Rain is precipitation that consists of drops of water. Raindrops form in clouds when microscopic droplets of water grow or when particles of ice melt before reaching the ground. In inland areas of Antarctica, all precipitation falls as snow. Rain does not fall evenly over the Earth. Some regions are always too dry, and others too wet. A region that usually gets enough rain may suddenly have a serious dry spell, and another region may be flooded with too much rain.

• FACT FILE •

The islands of the Seychelles are very humid and have high levels of rainfall, which feeds the tropical rainforests.
The average annual rainfall ranges from 132cm (52in) on some of the coral islands to 234cm (92in) on Mahé.

WHAT IS ACID RAIN?

Regions affected by acid rain include large parts of eastern North America, Scandinavia and Central Europe, and parts of Asia.

Acid rain is a term for rain, snow, sleet or other wet precipitation that is polluted by such acids as sulphuric acid and nitric acid. Acid rain harms thousands of lakes, rivers and streams worldwide, killing fish and other wildlife. It also damages buildings, bridges and statues. High concentrations of acid rain can harm forests and soil.

Acid rain forms when vaporized water in the air reacts with chemical compounds. These compounds, including sulphur dioxide and nitrogen oxides, come largely from the burning of coal, gasoline and oil. Most vehicles, factories and power plants burn such fuels for energy.

Since about the 1950s, the problem of acid rain has increased in rural areas. This has occurred because the use of taller smokestacks in urban areas has enabled the winds to transport pollutants further from their sources.

• FACT FILE •

Adding lime from quarries to lakes and rivers and their drainage areas temporarily neutralizes their acidity. But it may have harmful side effects.

WHERE DOES A HURRICANE BEGIN?

Devastation caused by Hurricane Sandy

WHEN HURRICANE SANDY HIT THE UNITED STATES IN 2014, IT CAUSED LOSS OF ELECTRIC POWER TO 7.5 MILLION PEOPLE!

Hurricanes form in the Atlantic and East Pacific Oceans, when the surface temperature of the ocean is at least 27°C (81°F) over a wide, deep area and the conditions in the atmosphere are right. Because they are fuelled by warm water, they lose their strength over land. They are divided into categories, with category 1 the least and category 5 the worst. As well as the high winds, damage is caused by hail, heavy rainfall that can cause mudslides, and storm surges, which cause flooding. In 2005, Hurricane Katrina's storm surge caused more damage than the winds when it breached the flood defences at New Orleans. Elsewhere such storms are called typhoons and tropical cyclones.

• FACT FILE •

Approximately 85 hurricanes, typhoons and tropical cyclones occur in a year throughout the world. Hurricanes are most common during the summer and early autumn.

WHAT IS
A TSUNAMI?

An artist's impression of a tsunami heading for land

Tsunami waves are also called seismic sea waves.

Earthquakes on the ocean floor can give a tremendous push to surrounding seawater and create one or more large, destructive waves called tsunamis. Tsunamis may build to heights of more than 30m (100ft) when they reach shallow water near shore. In the open ocean, tsunamis typically move at speeds of 800 to 970km (500 to 600 miles) per hour. They can travel great distances while diminishing little in size and can flood coastal areas thousands of miles from their source.

In 2004, the Indian Ocean Tsunami killed hundreds of thousands of people and destroyed the coastline. Another form of tsunami is called a storm surge. This is caused when a violent storm whips up huge waves. In 1970 a storm surge and cyclone hit Bangladesh, killing 266,000 people. A further 10,000 people were killed when another one struck in 1985.

• FACT FILE •

Probably the best-known gauge of earthquake intensity is the local Richter magnitude scale, developed in 1935 by United States seismologist Charles F. Richter.

WHAT ARE THE MOST EXTREME TEMPERATURES RECORDED?

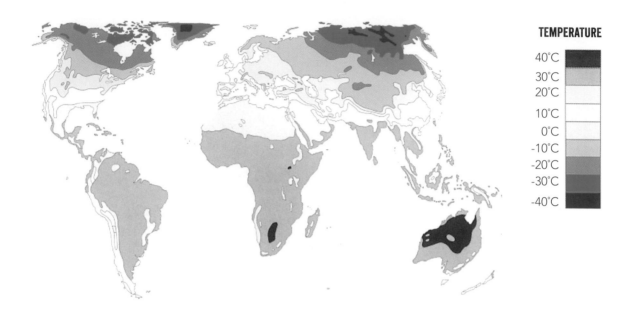

TEMPERATURE

40°C	
30°C	
20°C	
10°C	
0°C	
-10°C	
-20°C	
-30°C	
-40°C	

Libya and the Antarctic have recorded the most extreme temperatures. The hottest shade temperature was in Libya in 1922, when the temperature in the Sahara desert reached 58°C (136°F). Temperatures nearly as high as this were recorded in Death Valley in the USA in 1913. The coldest ever recorded temperature was in Antarctica in 1983, when Russian scientists measured a temperature low of –89.2°C (–128.6°F).

• FACT FILE •

Over millions of years the human body has altered to suit the climate of the regions we inhabit. In general, the hotter the region, the darker the skin of its inhabitants.

WHEN WAS THE LONGEST HEATWAVE?

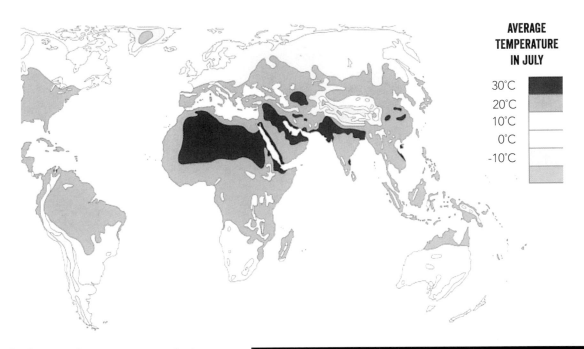

AVERAGE TEMPERATURE IN JULY

30°C
20°C
10°C
0°C
-10°C

The longest heatwave recorded was in Marble Bar, Australia when the temperature stayed above 38°C (100°F). It lasted for 162 days from 23 October 1923 to 7 April 1924.

The highest mean annual temperature recorded is 34.4°C (93.9°F) in Dallol, Ethiopia.

The lowest recorded temperature (outside of the poles) was −68°C (−90.4°F) in Verkhoyansk, Siberia, on 6 February 1933.

The lowest mean annual temperature of −56.6°C (−69.9°F) was recorded at the Plateau Station, Antarctica.

• FACT FILE •

Some living things have adapted to survive long periods of time without water. Plants such as cacti have the ability to conserve water. They also minimize water loss as they have no leaves, and photosynthesis takes place in the stem. They have roots which reach deep into the ground for water.

WHEN WAS THE LONGEST DROUGHT?

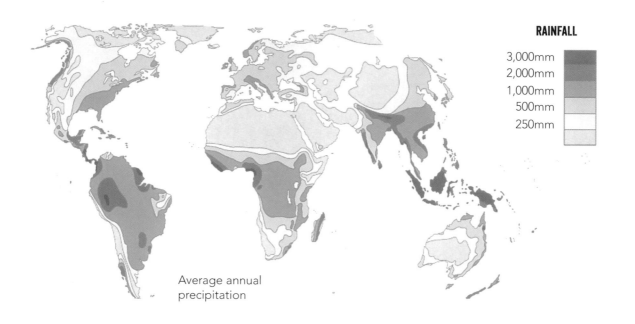

RAINFALL

3,000mm
2,000mm
1,000mm
500mm
250mm

Average annual precipitation

The longest drought in recorded history took place in Calama, in the Atacama Desert of Northern Chile. For four centuries, beginning in 1571, no rain fell in the area. It was not until 1971 that rainfall was first recorded again. The Atacama Desert, which lies between the Andes and the Pacific Ocean, is recognized as the driest place in the world.

The Atacama Desert remains so dry because it lies in a region where there is constant high air pressure, with little air movement, and with few clouds overhead.

• FACT FILE •

Some people believe that animals are good predictors of weather. One such belief is that if cows are standing in their field, then dry weather is expected. If they are lying down, however, rain is due.

WHAT CAUSES FLOODING?

A CAR CAN BE CARRIED AWAY IN AS LITTLE AS 60CM (2FT) OF WATER!

• FACT FILE •

Many of the world's cities are low lying and threatened by flooding. Bangkok, in Thailand, and Venice, in Italy (pictured here), are typical old cities built by water because they relied on shipping.

Flooding occurs when water cannot drain away fast enough in the rivers. In areas of non-porous rocks, water runs off the land very quickly and streams and rivers soon overflow. Flooding also happens when winter snows thaw in spring. Huge floods cover parts of Siberia every spring, when snow melts while the rivers are still iced up. Low-lying coastal lands are vulnerable to flooding, especially when gales and high tides cause water to flow inland. Low-lying Bangladesh is particularly liable to this kind of flooding. In addition, melting snow in the Himalayan mountains adds huge amounts of water to Bangladesh's rivers, increasing the flood risk.

WHY ARE
RAINFORESTS BEING CUT DOWN?

DID YOU KNOW THAT RAINFORESTS USED TO COVER 14 PER CENT OF THE EARTH'S SURFACE? TODAY THEY COVER ONLY AROUND 6 PER CENT.

• FACT FILE •

It is estimated that over two million different species of plant and animal thrive in the rainforests and many have been undiscovered by man. Their destruction is a serious threat to our planet.

Tropical rainforests contain the most varied mixtures of animals and plants of any habitat on the Earth. They contain large and small predators and a bewildering variety of birds. All these animals are supported by huge numbers of trees that produce fruit to feed them and their prey all year round. Unfortunately though, man is destroying their natural habitat. Rainforests are being cut down at an alarming rate, nearly 90 per cent of all rainforests have been destroyed. Both large commercial farming companies and individual farmers clear the forest to gain land to cultivate and graze animals. Secondly, trees have been felled to supply tropical hardwoods for furniture making and building.

WHY ARE MOST CORAL REEFS PROTECTED?

Coral reefs are the marine equivalent of rainforests. They are homes to thousands of species of fish and invertebrates, all living in a complex balance which makes the reef system an extremely stable environment. That is until the intervention of man.

Marine biologists spend a lot of time studying the reef and valuable new discoveries are made all the time. There are a great number of threats to coral reefs. Work must be done quickly to protect them. Therefore the education of people throughout the world is necessary if coral reefs are to survive.

• FACT FILE •

A starfish is one of the many thousands of sea creatures that make their home among the coral reefs. The starfish moves around on thousands of tiny tube feet. It also uses it feet to grab their prey of shellfish.

WHEN DO PONDS AND LAKES BECOME POLLUTED?

Many years ago the greatest threat to areas of standing water, such as ponds and lakes, was neglect. They gradually filled in and were occupied by shrubs and trees. Today, however, pollution from the modern world is the most serious threat to all water life. Farming practices pollute the water with fertilizers and pesticides. Sewage and waste from industry is also discharged into the rivers. On top of this, rivers and canals are often used as unofficial dumping sites for household waste. One of the saddest sights is to see dead fish floating on top of the water. Hopefully, tough laws controlling pollution may make this a thing of the past.

Ponds attract all manner of wildlife, including water beetles, newts, frogs, shrimps, dragonflies, mayflies and birds.

FACT FILE

Frogs produce large quantities of spawn in the spring. Keep a small amount in a jar with pond weeds and watch it grow into tadpoles.

WHAT IS IRRIGATION?

Irrigation is the watering of land by artificial methods. It provides water for plant growth in areas that have long periods of little or no rainfall. The water used for irrigation is taken from lakes, rivers, streams and wells.

Irrigation is used chiefly in three types of climates. In desert regions, such as Egypt and the southwestern United States, farming would be impossible without irrigation. In regions with seasonal rainfall, such as California and Italy, irrigation makes farming possible even during dry months.

DID YOU KNOW THAT THE ANCIENT EGYPTIANS DIVERTED WATER FROM THE RIVER NILE TO IRRIGATE THEIR LAND? THEY WERE ONE OF THE FIRST CIVILIZATIONS TO DO SO.

WHEN DOES THE APPEARANCE OF SOIL CHANGE?

Soil changes its appearance when the biological or chemical make-up of it varies. For example, red soil is found in areas where there is a high content of iron compounds. Oxisol is a good example of this; it is found in tropical regions where both chemical and biological activity are high. It is illustrated here (5).

The illustrations show different types of soil. You can see that the appearance changes enormously. 1 is tundra soil, which is very dark and peaty. 2 is soil belonging to desert regions; these areas tend to be unsuitable for plant growth, so this soil is lacking in nutrients and organic matter. The light-brown soils 3 and 4 are common in grassland areas. In contrast, soils 6, 7, 8 and 9 are typical of northern climates, where there is heavy rainfall and slow evaporation. These richer soils are suitable for plant growth.

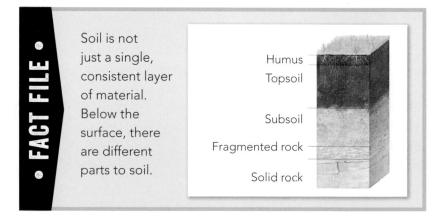

DIFFERENT TYPES OF SOIL

1 2 3
4 5 6
7 8 9

FACT FILE

Soil is not just a single, consistent layer of material. Below the surface, there are different parts to soil.

Humus
Topsoil
Subsoil
Fragmented rock
Solid rock

WHEN IS CLIMAX VEGETATION ACHIEVED?

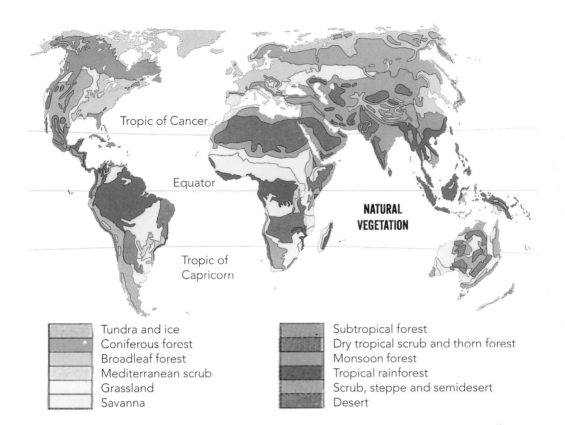

Tropic of Cancer

Equator

NATURAL VEGETATION

Tropic of Capricorn

Tundra and ice
Coniferous forest
Broadleaf forest
Mediterranean scrub
Grassland
Savanna

Subtropical forest
Dry tropical scrub and thorn forest
Monsoon forest
Tropical rainforest
Scrub, steppe and semidesert
Desert

When vegetation first starts growing in newly formed soil, it is at a disadvantage because the soil will not be nutrient-rich. As the plants die, they enrich the soil, allowing more plants to take advantage of this. As the soil gets older, it has gleaned more and more nutrients from dead plants – and more and more plants are able to grow successfully in the soil. Climax vegetation occurs when the vegetation is totally suited to the soil in the given climate. In reality, this can never last permanently due to the ever-changing environment.

• FACT FILE •

Rainforests have developed in areas where the soil is very fertile and where there is a great deal of rainfall. The varied vegetation suggests the soil is extremely nutrient-rich.

WHY ARE WIND TURBINES USED AS A POWER SOURCE?

When oil, gas and coal run out, people will need other sources of energy to fuel their cars and light their houses. Concerns about pollution resulting from the production of electrical power have led to the development of wind turbines. Huge windmills situated on exposed and windy areas are now a common sight in many parts of the world.

Strong, steady winds can be put to work turning windmill blades. As the blades spin, they turn a shaft that generates electricity. These modern wind turbines come in several shapes. Large groups of them are called wind farms. The windmills of a wind farm can power generators to produce electricity for many homes.

FACT FILE

The principle of the windmill has been known since ancient times, but little is known of its use before the 12th century. They were originally used to pump water for livestock, household use, or for irrigation.

THERE ARE MORE THAN 270,000 WIND TURBINES IN OPERATION ACROSS THE GLOBE!

WHY ARE SOLAR PANELS ATTACHED TO ROOFTOPS?

There is always a constant search for new sources of energy. The Sun gives out vast amounts of energy, of which only a tiny fraction reaches the Earth. If we could use just a small part of this energy it would fulfil all the world's foreseeable needs for power. One way of harnessing the Sun's power is by using solar panels. Today a number of houses generate some of their own power. Solar panels attached to rooftops absorb the Sun's energy, which is later used to heat domestic water supplies. The first solar power station was built in 1969 at Odeillo in France. It uses solar power to generate energy and has many solar panels to collect as much energy from the Sun as possible. One day scientists hope to collect sunlight in space and beam it back to Earth.

 DID YOU KNOW THAT NASA HAS BEEN DEVELOPING AN UNMANNED SOLAR-POWERED AIRCRAFT SINCE THE 1980s?

• FACT FILE •

The Sun's rays heat water in a pipe system within the solar panels. Cold water enters the pipes and flows through the panel, heating up as it goes. Hot water is collected from the pipes and stored for future use.

WHAT IS CONSERVATION?

Over the last few decades very large areas of natural habitats, once rich in plant and animal life, have disappeared under buildings, roads and farms. Modern farming methods, with large fields, intensive use of pesticides and high crop yields, do not give many wildflowers and animals a chance to survive. Nowadays, most species survive in places where these changes have not taken place – old woodland and heathland, for example. However, natural habitats are disappearing fast, and constant effort is needed to conserve what is left. Otherwise they may deteriorate so much that they become unsuitable for species that depend on them for survival.

WHAT IS POLLUTION?

Pollution is the name we give to waste products that enter the air, soil and water, but cannot be quickly broken down by natural processes. Instead they affect the health of plants and animals, including humans, and the environments they live in. Controlling the emissions of factories and vehicles can help. It is also important, as far as possible, to use materials that can break down in the soil when they are thrown away. Such materials are said to be biodegradable.

• FACT FILE •

Rivers and canals are often used as unofficial dumping sites for household waste. To improve matters, there are new laws to protect the environment. But we all need to help to keep the environment clean and healthy.

WHY ARE RHINOS BECOMING ENDANGERED?

Some animal species have become extinct because they are less successful than other species that gradually replace them. But this is not so in the case of the rhinoceros. Hunting is the reason for their reduced numbers. In fact poaching has reduced the numbers of black rhinos to around 2,500. Most survive today only in protected game parks. A rhino horn can grow as long as 157cm (62in).

? DID YOU KNOW THAT THE RED WOLF BECAME EXTINCT IN THE WILD IN 1980? SINCE THEN SMALL NUMBERS OF CAPTIVE SPECIMENS HAVE BEEN BRED AND THERE ARE NOW AROUND 200 IN CAPTIVITY.

HOW ENDANGERED ARE PANDAS?

There were never any great numbers of pandas but farming has now destroyed much of their natural habitat in China. Due to shortage of food there are now less than 1,000 giant pandas remaining.

Humans have accelerated the extinction of many more animals by changing their environment so rapidly that the animals do not have time to adapt. One example is the destruction of the Indonesian rainforest which has left nowhere for the orangutan to live. Hunting is another reason for the reduced number of animals such as tigers, and the likely extinction of others.

DID YOU KNOW THAT THE PANDA FEATURES AS THE SYMBOL OF THE WORLD WILDLIFE FUND? THE ORGANIZATION IS CONCERNED WITH HELPING ENDANGERED SPECIES.

• FACT FILE •

Millions of African elephants have been hunted down and killed by poachers for their ivory tusks. These elephants are becoming endangered.

THE
PLANT WORLD

CONTENTS

HOW DO TREES GROW?

Trees need nourishment to grow. They obtain water and minerals from the soil and carbon dioxide from the air. Chlorophyll in their leaves harnesses the energy of the Sun's rays to make sugar, starch and cellulose.

Between the wood of a tree and its bark, there is a thin band of living cells called the cambium. New cells are formed here; those that develop on the wood side of the cambium grow as wood and those on the bark side mature as bark. In this way, as the tree grows older it increases in diameter.

Trees grow in height as well as in diameter. At the end of each branch or twig there is a group of living cells. During periods of active growth, these cells multiply to form new leaves and stem length.

A cross-section of a tree shows alternating bands of light and dark wood. The lighter bands have bigger cells and were formed in spring; the dark bands consist of small, tightly packed cells made in the autumn.

Trees have wide-spreading roots underground. They can reach greater distances for water and vital nutrients and help keep the tree stable.

FACT FILE

Trees are the largest living organisms on Earth. The biggest tree, the Californian giant redwood, is nearly 100m (328ft) high and has a trunk that is 11m (36ft) thick. The total weight of one of these trees is more than 2,000 tonnes. These ancient trees have very few branches and leaves, and are often scarred by fire and lightning strikes.

WHY DO TREES HAVE BARK?

The outer layers of trees and woody shrubs are known as bark. Bark has a number of functions in protecting the tree: it gives added rigidity to the structure, insulates the delicate inner layers and helps to shield them from damage by insects and diseases. It also stops water evaporating: without it the cycle of water rising through the trunk and sugars passing down would falter.

Bark needs to be able to allow the tree trunk to expand as it grows year by year and some trees, such as silver birch, as well as some pines and stringy bark eucalyptus shed bits of their bark continually so that this can happen.

• FACT FILE •

The coconut is a large, hollow nut, which grows on a palm tree. It contains a milky fluid that you can drink. The white lining is also edible and used in cooking. The coconut fibres on the outside of the shell are used for making coconut matting and sacking.

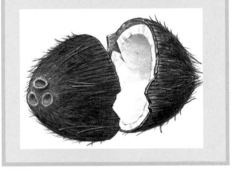

?

DID YOU KNOW THAT A TREE HAVING BARK IS LIKE YOU HAVING SKIN? THE BARK PROTECTS THE LIVING WOOD INSIDE FROM EXTREME WEATHER. IT HAS TINY HOLES IN IT SO THAT OXYGEN CAN ENTER THE TRUNK AND CARBON DIOXIDE CAN LEAVE IT.

HOW DO PINE TREES STAY GREEN ALL YEAR?

Leaves have several functions and one of them is to make food for the tree. Leaves take in carbon dioxide from the air and water and minerals from the soil. The chlorophyll in the leaves absorbs energy from the Sun. Sunshine forces the chlorophyll to change the carbon dioxide and water into sugar. The sugar made in the leaves is the tree's food.

Leaves also give off enormous quantities of water. Certain trees, however, like pines and firs have different kinds of leaves. They have narrow, needle-like leaves with a thick, waxy outer covering which prevents the evaporation of water. Consequently the leaves on such trees remain for several years. When the leaves do fall, new ones grow at the same time and the branches never look bare. That is why these types of trees are called evergreens.

Corsican Pine

Norway Spruce

THERE ARE AROUND 100 HUNDRED DIFFERENT TYPES OF PINE TREE! THEY INCLUDE THE WHITEBARK PINE, THE FOXTAIL PINE, THE SWISS PINE, THE CUBAN PINE, THE MOUNTAIN PINE AND THE MARITIME PINE.

WHY DOES A PINE TREE HAVE CONES?

THE BIGGEST PINE CONES GROW AS LONG AS 40CM (16IN) AND CAN WEIGH UP TO 4.5KG (10LB). THEY COME FROM THE COULTER PINE, WHICH GROWS IN SOUTHERN CALIFORNIA.

A pine tree has cones in order to reproduce. The pine cone is actually a highly modified branch that takes the place of a flower. Separate male cones and female seed cones are borne on the same tree. Each of the numerous scales of the male cone bears pollen, while each female cone scale bears ovules in which egg cells are produced. In the pine, the male cones are small and short-lived, and are borne in clusters at the top of the tree. At the time of pollination, enormous numbers of pollen grains are released and dispersed by the wind. Those that land accidentally on female cone scales extend pollen tubes part way into the ovule during one growing season but usually do not reach the stage of actual fertilization until the next year. The cones that are usually seen are the seed cones, which are normally hard and woody.

• FACT FILE •

Scots pine trees need to be tough to survive long winters. They have thousands of tiny, needle-like leaves that have a waterproof coating to protect them from the rain and snow.

WHAT IS THE FRUIT OF THE OAK?

The acorn is the fruit of the oak tree. In the spring, oaks produce small, yellowish-green flowers. The male flowers, which form in dangling clusters called catkins, produce large amounts of pollen. The wind carries the pollen to the female flowers and fertilizes them. Once fertilized, a female flower will become an acorn. Acorns vary in length from less than 13mm (½in) to more than 5cm (2in). Oaks grow slowly and usually do not bear acorns until they are about 20 years old. Most oaks live for 200 to 400 years.

? DID YOU KNOW THAT THE ENGLISH OAK IS THE MOST COMMON TREE FOUND GROWING IN THE UNITED KINGDOM?

WHY DO PLANTS HAVE ROOTS?

Light energy from the Sun

Water is taken in by the roots

• FACT FILE •

Some plants, such as carrots and swede, are grown for their swollen edible taproots, which they use to store energy.

There are two main reasons: to provide stability and to obtain water and nutrients. There are two common types of root system: taproots, where the plant has one major root with others branching off from it and fibrous roots, where lots of smaller roots spread through the soil directly from the bottom of the plant's stem.

There are some plants that do not use their roots to obtain food, these include carnivorous plants, such as the venus fly trap, and 'epiphytic' plants that absorb nutrients through their leaves from the air, including the 'air plants' from South America.

HOW DO LEAVES GROW?

Green plants and trees have to manufacture their food. The leaves are the food factories for plants and trees.

Leaves of fruit trees manufacture food that helps them to make fruit. For example, peaches are sweet. So peach tree leaves make sugar. By a process called photosynthesis, leaves manufacture sugar from the water and carbon dioxide. Leaves are able to carry out these processes because of chloroplasts, which contain chlorophyll, inside their cells.

The roots of a plant or tree take water from the soil that eventually reaches the veins of the leaves. These veins carry back food the leaves have made. Carbon dioxide enters the tree's cells through the leaves and when the Sun is shining, leaves manufacture the sugar. In doing so, oxygen is produced which exits the tree through its leaves.

Leaves give off water, too. Part of the water taken in through the root is used to make sugar. The rest is given off through the surface of the leaves.

• FACT FILE •

Energy from the Sun evaporates water from the leaf surface, through the stomata. This reduces pressure in the channels carrying water from the roots, so more water is drawn up the stem.

HOW DO
LEAF SHAPES VARY?

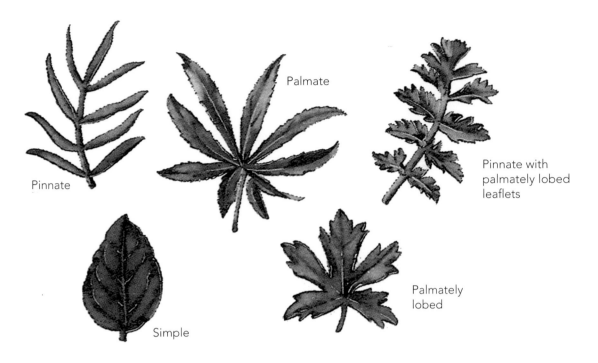

Palmate

Pinnate

Pinnate with palmately lobed leaflets

Simple

Palmately lobed

The shapes of plant leaves vary considerably. The edges of leaves may be smooth or jagged. The leaf blades may be undivided (simple), or they may be divided (lobed) in various ways. Some leaves may be made up of separate leaflets. The commonest leaf shapes are shown above.

The leaves themselves may be arranged on the plant in different ways, and this is usually standard for any given type of plant. A leaf arrangement that has single leaves at each level is called alternate. Leaves arranged in pairs are known as opposite. Opposite leaves may all face the same way, or each pair may be set at right angles to the pair below.

• FACT FILE •

Some plants have all their leaves in a ring at the base of the stem. This is known as a rosette.

WHAT ARE STOMATA?

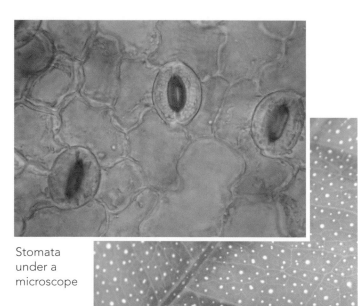

Stomata under a microscope

Stomata on a lime leaf

Stomata are tiny holes in leaves, which a plant can open and close. When the stomata are open, they let air in and out and water out. When the stomata are closed, water cannot escape from the leaves.

Plants absorb water from the soil through their roots. This water moves up the stem to the leaves, where about 90 per cent evaporates through the stomata. Large trees lose more than 800 litres (200 gallons) of water from their leaves each day. This loss of water from leaves by evaporation is called transpiration. Other plant processes that involve water include photosynthesis, which uses water to make food, and respiration, in which water is produced. When it is dark, plants shut down for the night by closing their stomata.

FACT FILE

Every day, a large tree loses enough water for you to take eight long showers. About 99 per cent of the water absorbed by the roots is lost by the leaves in transpiration.

HOW CAN LEAVES CHANGE THEIR COLOUR?

When we look at a tree in summertime we only see one colour: green. And yet in the autumn these same leaves take on a whole variety of colours. The green colour in leaves is due to chlorophyll. There are other colours present in a leaf but we cannot normally see them. The pigment 'xanthopyll' makes yellow, 'carotin' orange and 'anthocyanin' is a bright red colour.

In the summer we only see the chlorophyll, but as the weather starts turning colder the food that has been stored away in the leaves starts to flow out to the branches and trunk. Since no more food will be produced in the winter, the chlorophyll food factory closes down and disintegrates. As the chlorophyll disappears, the other pigments that have been present all the time become visible. So the leaves take on all those beautiful colours that we enjoy seeing.

New England in the United States is famous for its autumn colour as billions of leaves change from green to a kaleidoscope of colours.

WHY ARE THERE SO MANY FLOWER SHAPES?

The reason that flowers come in so many different shapes and colours is to help ensure that they are fertilized. Flowers that rely on insects for pollination must make sure that the insect is carrying pollen from the same kind of plant. The shape of the flower ensures that only certain kinds of insect can pollinate it. Flat flowers, such as daisies and sunflowers, can be visited by hoverflies and some bees. Flowers that are formed into tubes only attract insects that have long tongues.

FACT FILE

Bees are attracted to the colour and scent of a flower. They feed on the nectar in the flower and gather pollen, which they store in sacs on their legs.

?

DID YOU KNOW THAT FLOWERS DID NOT ALWAYS EXIST? THERE WAS A TIME WHEN FERNS AND CONE-BEARING TREES DOMINATED THE EARTH. BUT THAT WAS 140 MILLION YEARS AGO!

HOW ARE FLOWERS ARRANGED?

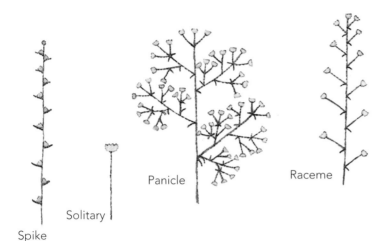

Panicle

Raceme

Solitary

Spike

Single umbel

Cyme

Flowers are produced in many different arrangements on different plants. Solitary flowers are borne singly, with one flower on each stem. Other arrangements are far more complex. A group of flowers together on one plant is called an inflorescence. The patterns of the branching flowers in an inflorescence tend to be the same for a given type of plant. The most common flower arrangements are shown here.

ONE OF THE LARGEST FLOWERS IN THE WORLD BELONGS TO A PLANT CALLED THE PUYA RAIMONDII. ITS FLOWER STALK GROWS TO 9M (29.5FT) TALL AND MIGHT HAVE AS MANY AS 3,000 BLOOMS.

HOW DO FLOWERS DEVELOP THEIR SCENT?

A flower has a fragrance when certain essential oils are found in the petals. These oils are produced by the plant as part of its growing process. They are very complex and under certain conditions this substance is broken down or decomposed and is formed into a volatile oil. This oil evaporates and when this happens we can smell the fragrance it gives off.

The type of scent a flower gives off depends on the different chemicals in the volatile oil. Various combinations produce different fragrances. These same oils can also be found in leaves, bark, roots, fruit and seeds. As an example, oranges and lemons have them in their fruit, almonds in their seeds and cinnamon in its bark.

The Arabians were the first to distil rose petals with water to produce rose water. This was 1,200 years ago, and we still extract perfume from flowers today.

FACT FILE

The hummingbird is the world's smallest bird. It can hover backwards as it feeds on flower nectar.

?

DID YOU KNOW THAT THERE IS A FLOWER THAT SMELLS OF ROTTING BODIES? IT IS EVEN CALLED A CORPSE FLOWER AND SMELLS THAT WAY IN ORDER TO ATTRACT FLIES TO HELP IT POLLINATE.

WHY ARE SOME FLOWERS VERY COLOURFUL?

A flower is the means by which a plant reproduces. It contains male or female organs, or both together. Flowers usually have brightly coloured petals or sepals. The reason that flowers are so brightly coloured and perfumed is to attract insects. Insects play a very important part in pollinating them.

Some plants also produce a sugary liquid called nectar, which attracts the bees. As they fly from flower to flower the insects transfer the pollen to the stigma of the flower and fertilize it.

 THERE ARE AS MANY AS 400,000 SPECIES OF FLOWERING PLANT IN THE WORLD! ROSES HAVE 100 SPECIES ALONE.

• FACT FILE •

Did you know that the bat's long tongue is perfect for whisking out the nectar from a flower? Pollen is brushed onto the bat's fur as it moves from flower to flower.

WHAT IS POLLEN?

Pollen comes in many vibrant colours that include yellow, green, red, purple, white and brown.

Pollen is the plant's equivalent of an animal's sperm: it carries the male reproductive genes. Pollen consists of tiny grains, each with a tough coat that is often patterned with characteristic ridges and spikes. When inhaled, the fine pollen causes allergies such as hay fever in some susceptible people. Pollen can be found in fossil deposits, making it possible to identify the plants that were living millions of years ago – even though no actual plant fossils may be found. Pollination takes place when a pollen grain is deposited on the tip of a pistil. It then grows a long tube down inside the pistil that fuses with the egg cell and completes the process of fertilization.

• FACT FILE •

Bees are attracted to the shape and scent of a flower. They feed on the nectar in the flower and gather pollen, which they store in sacs on their legs to take back to the hive.

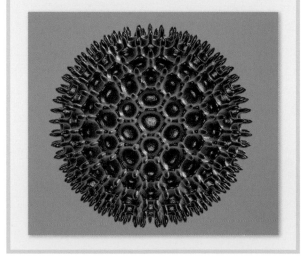

WHEN DOES POLLINATION TAKE PLACE?

Pollination is the process of transferring pollen from the stamen to the stigma. It is possible for flowers to pollinate themselves, or other flowers on the same plant – this is called self-pollination. It is, however, much better for the health of the species if cross-pollination occurs – that is, if pollen is transferred from one plant to another. The most common method involves insects that are attracted to the flowers for their nectar. Pollen grains stick to the insects' bodies and are effectively transferred from one plant to another as the insect moves from flower to flower. Other, less attractive types of flower, use wind to transport their pollen.

ANATOMY OF A FLOWER

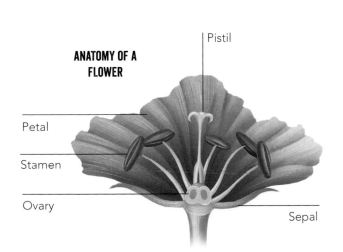

Pistil

Petal

Stamen

Ovary

Sepal

The flowers of orchids are highly specialized for pollination by insects. When the insect pushes into the flower to reach the nectar, the pollinia stick onto its head.

HOW DO FERNS REPRODUCE?

Ferns do not reproduce in the same way as other plants. They have fronds instead of true leaves, and some ferns grow into a tree-like form that can be 24m (78.7ft) tall.

Microscopic spores are produced on the underside of the fronds and these are scattered by the wind. When these spores land in a suitably damp place, they sprout and grow into a tiny flat plant that develops small reproductive structures.

Sperm fertilizes the egg cell, which begins to grow as the tiny plant shrivels up and dies. This is when the complete fern begins to develop.

The fern's reproductive parts are very delicate and can only survive in a moist atmosphere, so these plants will only grow in damp places.

Ferns grow all over the world, in damp shady places, such as forests, fields and swamps. In all, there are around 12,000 species of fern.

FACT FILE

Seaweed is a from of algae—one of planet Earth's most primitive types of plant. Algae can grow up to several metres in length. These plants do not have roots but grip to the surface with an organ called a holdfast.

WHAT ARE UMBELS?

The carrot family, or Umbelliferae, all have flowers that are arranged in umbels, or like the spokes of an upside-down umbrella. Often each ray of the umbel has another smaller umbel on it, making a compound umbel with numerous flowers. Ivy is in a closely related family and also has umbels of flowers, but its fruits are round and fleshy.

One of the most commonly found plants with umbels is cow parsley, where its masses of white flowers are a familiar sight on the roadside in England in spring months.

Cow parsley

Ivy

• FACT FILE •

Some of our familiar vegetables, such as parsnip and carrot, have been developed from wild plants of this family.

WHAT ARE SUCCULENTS?

Succulents are plants that have leaves, stems or roots that can store water so that they can survive extended periods of drought. All the plants in the cactus family are considered stem succulents. During periods of moisture, their stems swell and then during droughts they slowly contract. Cacti with ribs are particularly well adapted to surviving droughts as their ribs expand and contract like an accordion. Cacti get their name from the Greek word *kaktos* meaning thistle.

The name 'succulent' comes from the Latin word *sucus*, which means juice or sap.

WHAT ARE LICHENS?

Lichens are peculiar organisms in which algae and fungi live together. They are usually flat and crust-like, with no roots and often grow on roofs, rocks or tree branches. Some grow like a small branched tree, while others can be found hanging from tree branches. The main structure of a lichen is the fungal part, but it also contains algae cells which contribute food through photosynthesis. Lichens grow very slowly, but can eventually cover very large areas.

 LICHENS GROWING ON ROCKS IN ANTARCTICA ARE THOUGHT TO BE 10,000 YEARS OLD – THEY ARE THE OLDEST LIVING ORGANISMS!

• FACT FILE •

Reindeer moss is a form of lichen that is very common throughout the Arctic. It forms the main diet of the caribou and other grazing animals.

WHAT ARE ALGAE?

Algae are the most primitive forms of plant life. Most algae are aquatic, and they range in size from microscopic single-celled organisms to seaweed that is several metres long. Algae photosynthesize, like other plants, and they are responsible for providing most of the world's oxygen. Algae are very varied, but even the large forms, such as kelp and other seaweeds, lack the true leaves, stems and roots found in other plants. Not all algae use the green chlorophyll found in other plants in order to photosynthesize, some use red or brown pigments for this purpose.

DID YOU KNOW THAT YOU CAN EAT SEAWEED? KINDS THAT PEOPLE EAT INCLUDE DULSE, SEA GRAPES, SEA LETTUCE, BLADDERWRACK, KOMBU, NORI AND LAVER.

FACT FILE

Giant kelp looks like a kind of seaweed, but it is in fact the largest-known kind of algae. It grows in very long strands up to 65m (213ft) in length, and is fastened to the seabed with a root-like organ called a holdfast.

WHAT IS A WEED?

Dandelion

Bindweed

Nettle

A weed is any plant that grows where people do not want it to grow. A plant may be considered a weed in one place, but not necessarily in another. Some plants such as poison ivy are called weeds wherever they grow because they have no known use. Many weeds are destructive. These species reduce both the quality and quantity of crops by competing with them for sunlight, water and nourishing substances in the soil. Some types of weed also shelter insects and diseases that damage nearby crops. Weeds including nettles and poison ivy produce skin reactions in most people if brushed up against.

FACT FILE

Weeds can also be beneficial. For example, they reduce the erosion on land where cultivated plants do not grow. They also provide shelter and food for birds and other wildlife. Fireweed, pictured here, is one of many weeds used in making medicines to relieve pain.

WHERE DO CACTI GROW IN THE WILD?

Cacti are native to North and South America and the West Indies, but now grow widely across the world, even Alaska. They spread to Spain, and then across the Mediterranean, following the Spanish conquest of South America.

What all cacti have in common is that they store water in their stems and have structures called areoles from which their spines, branches (if they have them) and flowers – which are adapted leaves – emerge.

Cacti come in many shapes and sizes from the branched opuntias and organ-pipe cacti, to the barrel-shape of mammilaria.

FACT FILE

The liquid inside a cactus is not pure, clear water but a thick viscous liquid. It is drinkable and has saved many lives in the desert.

Not all cacti originate in deserts. Some, such as the Christmas cactus, come from Brazilian rainforests.

WHAT ARE FUNGI?

Fungi used to be considered a part of the plant kingdom, but they are now thought to be quite different. The main part of the fungus is a mass of tiny threads called mycelium. Fungi live on other organic matter. In the soil, fungi are the most important agent in the breakdown of dead plant and animal material, recycling it so that plants can use the nutrients. Fungi live in damp areas or in water because they have no method of preventing their fragile threads from drying out – they cannot survive dry atmospheres.

THERE ARE AROUND 50,000 SPECIES OF FUNGI AND THEY INCLUDE YEAST, RUSTS, SMUTS, MILDEWS, MOULDS AND MUSHROOMS.

• FACT FILE •

Fungi have been a popular food for hundreds of years, even as far back as Roman times. A number of species such as the truffle, cep and mushroom are delicious and safe to eat. A great many are not edible.

WHEN DO
PLANTS EAT INSECTS?

Plants growing in bogs and peaty areas often need to supplement their food supply by catching insects. Bog water contains very little nitrogen, but some bog plants can obtain this substance by catching and digesting insects. They are known as insectivorous plants. Other insectivorous plants are covered with sticky tentacles that trap flies. The most remarkable is the Venus flytrap plant. It has two clawed plates that slam together when a fly walks over them and touches a trigger hair. Other insect-eating plants are aquatic, catching tiny crustaceans in bladder-shaped underwater traps. Some of the largest insectivorous plants live in the tropical rainforests.

BLADDERWORTS LIVE BESIDE PONDS AND HAVE TRAPS – CALLED BLADDER TRAPS – IN WHICH THEY CAN CATCH PREY. SOME TRAPS ARE BIG ENOUGH TO CATCH SMALL TADPOLES!

• FACT FILE •

Some insects use camouflage to blend into their environment, protecting themselves from predators.

HOW DID THE TIGER LILY GET ITS NAME?

The tiger lily is a tall, hardy garden flower named for its black-spotted, reddish-orange petals, which resemble a tiger's pelt. A few varieties have red, white or yellow petals. Tiger lily stems are greenish-purple or dark brown, and many grow from 1.2 to 1.5m (4 to 5ft) high. There may be as many as 20 flowers on a stem. The leaves are long and spear-shaped.

Tiger lily plants grow from bulbs. Tiny black bulbils (bulblets) develop where the leaves join the stalk. The bulbils eventually drop off, producing new plants. Tiger lilies grow best in bright sunlight and in well-drained, slightly acid soil.

• FACT FILE •

Magnolia trees are one of the oldest flowering plants. They have been around for one hundred million years, and are still flourishing today.

The lily first grew in China, Japan and Korea but has become a popular garden plant in North America and Europe.

WHERE WAS THYME FIRST USED?

Today, thyme is used as a kitchen herb, but originally the dried leaves were burned in temples in ancient Greece to create an incense in religious ceremonies. The plants are native to the Mediterranean region and there are about 300 to 400 species, a few of which are used in cooking, including common thyme and lemon thyme. Common thyme has hairy stems and paired elliptical leaves and its flowers are usually lilac and form in circles round the stems. It is a member of the mint family and is popular in many savoury dishes.

The essential oil in thyme is used in aromatherapy as an antiseptic and the extract thymol is used in a number of simple medicines such as cough mixture.

FACT FILE

Rosemary is an evergreen shrub of the mint family noted for the fragrance of its leaves. Rosemary is used fresh or dried as a herb for cooking. The plant also yields an oil used in perfumes.

WHERE DID THE NAME BUTTERCUP COME FROM?

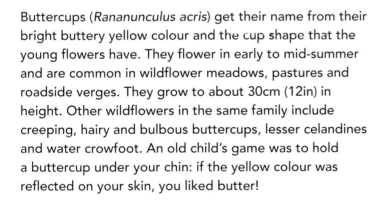

Buttercups (*Rananunculus acris*) get their name from their bright buttery yellow colour and the cup shape that the young flowers have. They flower in early to mid-summer and are common in wildflower meadows, pastures and roadside verges. They grow to about 30cm (12in) in height. Other wildflowers in the same family include creeping, hairy and bulbous buttercups, lesser celandines and water crowfoot. An old child's game was to hold a buttercup under your chin: if the yellow colour was reflected on your skin, you liked butter!

? DID YOU KNOW THAT BUTTERCUPS CAN BE POISONOUS? THEY HAVE A SOUR TASTE, WHICH MAKES ANIMALS LESS LIKELY TO EAT THEM.

• FACT FILE •

Strangely, cows do not eat buttercups because of their acrid taste, so farmers look on them as weeds. They can quickly take over an area because they spread so rapidly and grow faster than other flowers so they get the lion's share of the light.

WHERE WOULD YOU FIND A KOLA NUT?

Kola nuts are the seeds from the fruit of 125 species of tree from the tropical rainforests of West Africa, which are now also widely cultivated in South America, the Caribbean and Asia. The nuts are either white or red and are irregularly shaped. They contain caffeine and theobromine, which are mild stimulants and the extract from the nuts is used in soft drinks such as colas and in medicines such as pain killers and cold remedies.

In western Africa, they are often used as ceremonial gifts and in the past were chewed both for their mildly stimulant effect and because they could remove hunger pangs.

Kola nut

FACT FILE

Most nuts are rich in protein and fat, though chestnuts and a few others have more starch than protein. In Italy, bread is sometimes baked with a flour made from chestnuts.

?

DID YOU KNOW THAT THE FIRST COLA DRINK WAS MADE USING A COMBINATION OF COCA AND KOLA NUTS?

WHERE DOES A COCONUT GROW?

Coconuts originally grew only in Southeast Asia and Melanesia, but now they are grown across all areas of the world that are warm enough. They often grow next to the coast of tropical islands as seeds from other coconut trees have been carried there by the ocean currents.

Coconuts grow in clusters among the feathery fronds at the top of coconut trees. The large green husk and rind surround the hard, brown shell, inside which are the white coconut meat and the thin liquid called coconut milk.

In coconut plantations, the nuts are harvested several times a year, but will fall naturally after about a year when they are ripe. Products that are made from the flesh include copra, desiccated coconut, creamed coconut and coconut milk. The husk is used to make ropes, mats and plant compost.

In some countries, coconut farmers train monkeys to harvest coconuts for them. Coconut trees can be tall and dangerous to climb, and monkeys have greater climbing skills than humans.

• FACT FILE •

The peanut plant is unusual because its pods develop underground. For this reason peanuts are often called groundnuts. Peanuts are a nutritious food. There are more energy-giving calories in roasted peanuts than in the equivalent weight of steak.

WHAT ARE PERENNIAL PLANTS?

Perennial plants survive from one year to the next. They usually grow quite slowly, and can afford to build up their strength before they need to produce seeds. The parts of perennial plants that are above the ground are generally killed by frost in the autumn, but the roots and/or underground parts live through the winter. Growth is renewed and the cycle begins anew in the spring.

Perennial plants that grow in arid or desert conditions commonly survive dry times by becoming physiologically inactive. In some cases they remain alive but are dehydrated until water becomes available, at which time they rapidly absorb moisture through above-ground parts, swelling and resuming physiological activity. Some plants can absorb dew, which for many is the main water source. Mosses and lichens adopt this strategy, as do some flowering plants.

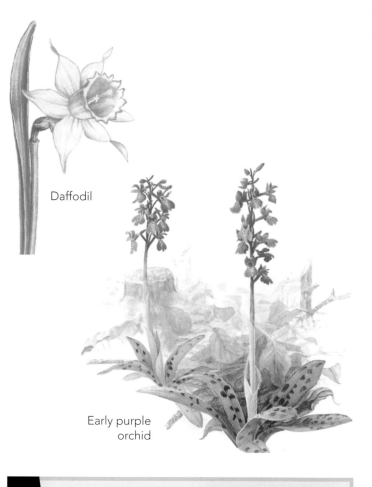

Daffodil

Early purple orchid

WHAT ARE BONSAI TREES?

Bonsai trees are decorative miniature trees or shrubs. The art originated in China, where, perhaps over 1,000 years ago, trees were cultivated in trays, wooden containers and earthenware pots and trained into naturalistic shapes. Bonsai, however, has been pursued and developed primarily by the Japanese.

They are dwarfed by a system of pruning roots and branches and training branches by tying them with wire. Some of these trees are very old and are perfect miniatures, even producing tiny flowers or cones.

• FACT FILE •

The Japanese are known for their liking of ornate plants and gardens. Even as far back as 700 CE, the Japanese developed beautiful gardens to enjoy.

The different styles of bonsai include slanted, upright, forest, cascade, broom, formal and informal.

MAMMALS,
REPTILES, AMPHIBIANS

CONTENTS

WHAT ARE MAMMALS?

Mammals are vertebrate animals who nourish their young with milk. All mammals and birds are warm-blooded. Most mammals have hair on their bodies that moults to be thin in the summer and thick in the winter. They also have a big brain inside their alert head, which enables them to learn quickly from experience, and retain memory so that they can undertake quite complicated tasks, such as finding a safe home and food. They have a strong internal skeleton of bones, including toes on four limbs, plus a tail, which, like the ears, can be very obvious. They can control their body heat over a wide range of weather conditions. Mammals have adapted to life in woodland, rivers, estuaries, seas, land, air, mountains and even the desert.

 **DID YOU KNOW THAT THE BLUE WHALE IS THE LARGEST OF ALL MAMMALS? IN FACT, IT IS THE LARGEST CREATURE EVER TO HAVE LIVED ON EARTH.**

• FACT FILE •

The female of any mammal, like the dog shown here, has the vital role of rearing the next generation. A typical feature is her milk or mammary glands with which to feed her young. That's where the name 'mammal' comes from.

WHAT ARE PRIMATES?

There are about 180 different species of primate, most of them living in the tropical regions of the world. The most numerous primate is *Homo sapiens* – the human being. All primates have fairly large brains and forward-facing eyes that enable them to judge distances accurately. Instead of claws or hoofs, like other mammals, they have fingers and toes with soft, sensitive tips. They also have the ability to grasp with their fingers, thumbs and toes. The largest primate is the gorilla. A male can weigh up to 274kg (605lb). The smallest is the mouse lemur, which has a total body length of only 12.5cm (6in).

Primates are classified as belonging to one of two groups – the wet-nosed primates or the dry-nosed primates.

• FACT FILE •

The gibbon is a small, man-like ape, found in Indo-Malayan forests. Gibbons, unlike the great apes, have elongated arms and hard, calloused skin on their buttocks. They have canine teeth and live in trees.

WHAT IS AN INVERTEBRATE?

An invertebrate is an animal without a backbone, and they make up 97 per cent of all animals. This group of animals includes all the arthropods such as spiders, insects and crustaceans. The remaining invertebrates are mainly soft-bodied animals, although many of them have shells. They include animals such as sponges, corals, shellfish, worms, sea urchins and starfish, and many less familiar animals. One invertebrate, the octopus, has proved to be highly intelligent when studied in the laboratory. Experiments have shown that it can recognize shapes and can remember different experiences.

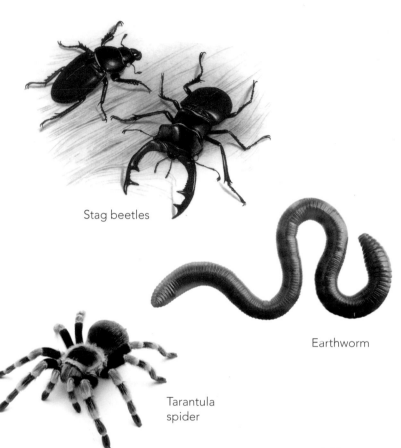

Stag beetles

Earthworm

Tarantula spider

FACT FILE

Assassin bugs are well named. They attack other insects and suck their body fluids. Caterpillars and grubs are a popular food because they have soft bodies and often no means of defence.

MANY OF THE WORLD'S PARASITES ARE INVERTEBRATES. THEY INCLUDE TICKS, TAPEWORMS AND LEECHES!

WHERE DO DOGS COME FROM?

Jack Russell

All the living members of the dog family are descended from a wolf-like creature called *tomarctus*. This ancient canine, called 'the father of dogs', roamed the Earth's forests perhaps 15 million years ago. The characteristics and habits of the wild dogs are all shared by the domestic dog. Domestic dogs are brothers under the skin to wolves, coyotes and jackals – the typical wild dogs. All belong to the branch of the dog family called *Canis*. A long time ago early man tamed a few wild dogs. These dogs may have been wolf cubs, jackals or some other member of the wild dog family. People found that these animals could be useful. They used them to help catch other animals and birds for food and clothing.

DID YOU KNOW THAT DOGS HAVE A GOOD VOCABULARY? THE AVERAGE DOG GENUINELY RECOGNIZES AROUND 150 DIFFERENT WORDS.

FACT FILE

As people became more civilized they discovered that the dog was a good friend and a helpful guard for home and cattle. Over the years, breeders have developed around 400 different dog breeds.

WHERE WOULD YOU SEE WILD CATS?

Wild cats can live between two and ten years, often in groups called colonies.

Wild cats have been forced, through hunting, to live in remote mountain forest areas. They can be found today in parts of southern and Central Europe, with a slowly recovering population in Scotland. They make their dens under fallen trees, among rocks or in vacated burrows. Wild cats are about twice the size of a domestic cat, and they also have a thicker, blunt-ended tail. They are shy, nocturnal animals and stay alone except during courtship in early spring. Their diet consists mainly of small mammals, birds and amphibians.

• FACT FILE •

Wild cats have been known to interbreed with domestic cats, especially when the wild cat lives near human habitation.

WHERE WOULD
YOU SEE A WILD BOAR?

AN ADULT MALE
CAN WEIGH UP TO
180KG (400LB)!

Wild boar used to be common in forests and dense woodland across much of Europe but most of them have been hunted. However, they can still be seen in some areas of southern France and northern Italy, as well as in the forests of Eastern Europe. They are also kept for hunting on some large estates. Wild boars were accidentally reintroduced into southern England when some escaped from a boar farm when a bad storm damaged their pens.

Wild boars feed at night and sleep during the day. Despite their large size they are usually shy animals and avoid human contact if they can. However, if they are cornered or, especially, if their young are threatened, they can be ferocious.

• FACT FILE •

No other hoofed animal in Europe makes a nest. Although the nest is simple, it does serve to protect the striped piglets for the first few days of life. They gradually lose their stripes as they mature.

WHY DOES A GIRAFFE HAVE A LONG NECK?

The giraffe is the tallest of all living animals. The strange shape and build of the giraffe is perfectly suited to enable it to obtain its food. A giraffe only eats plants, so its great height means it can reach the leaves on trees that grow in tropical lands where there is little grass.

A giraffe's tongue can be 46cm (18in) long and it uses it so skilfully that it can pick the smallest leaves off thorny plants without being pricked. It also has a long upper lip, which helps it wrench off many leaves at a time.

If a giraffe wants to take a drink from the ground, it has to adopt a peculiar stance by spreading its legs far apart in order to be able to reach down.

FACT FILE

The elephant is also an unusual animal, because of its very long trunk. The trunk is an extension of the nose and upper lip and serves the elephant as hand, arm, nose and lips all at once.

A GIRAFFE MIGHT HAVE A LONG NECK – AROUND 1.5M (5FT) – BUT IT HAS EXACTLY THE SAME NUMBER OF VERTEBRAE AS A HUMAN NECK!

WHY ARE
BEARS DANGEROUS?

There are eight bear species in the world, among them, the American black bear, the brown bear, the polar bear and the giant panda.

Bears can be 3m (9.10ft) tall and usually have thick, shaggy coats. Bears actually look very cuddly, but they can be very fierce. They are good tree climbers, powerful, quick to react and relatively harmless to people except when provoked, cornered or injured. Sometimes they can be a problem just through sheer friendliness.

In national parks, where they are familiar with human beings and come begging for food, visitors to the parks must keep to the protection of cars to avoid accidental injury from the bears' claws. Also, with their big strong arms, bears could hug a person to death. Some brown bears are affectionately known as 'grizzly' bears. The reason for this is because the tips of their brown hairs are grey, or grizzled.

• FACT FILE •

Many bears have rotten teeth. This is because they love sweet foods. One of their favourite foods is honey, which they steal from bees' nests high up in trees.

WHY IS THE LION CALLED 'KING OF THE BEASTS'?

Throughout history the lion has been considered the symbol of strength. In courts all over the world the lion was used on shields and crests and banners to indicate power. The lion's voice is a roar or a growl. The ancient Egyptians believed the lion was sacred, and during the time when Christ was born, lions lived in many parts of Europe. Today, the only places where lions are plentiful are in Africa.

The lion is just one of a group of animals known as big cats. Others include the tiger, the leopard, the snow leopard, the cheetah and the jaguar.

• FACT FILE •

Lions and tigers are thought of as the greatest cats of the wild. Stripy tigers and lions never meet in the wild; lions are native to Africa and stripy tigers are native to Asia.

HOW LONG CAN A CAMEL GO WITHOUT WATER?

The most important part of the camel is its hump. When that hump is empty, it loses its firm shape and flops to one side. The purpose of the hump is to serve as a storage place for food.

The camel can also take its own water supply along. The camel has three stomachs. It uses the first one to store food while it is grazing and to form it into cud. In the second stomach are the digestive juices and the chewed cud is digested in the third stomach.

In the walls of the first two stomachs, there are pockets for storing water. Muscles hold these pockets closed when they are full. Whenever the camel needs some water, these muscles open and close to let out as much water as it needs.

 IF A CAMEL TRAVELS SLOWLY AND WITH A LIGHT LOAD, THE WATER IN ITS STOMACH CAN LAST ANYTHING FROM SIX TO TEN DAYS!

FACT FILE

Plants can also store food and water over the winter or in very dry conditions. Underground storage organs develop from roots, stems or leaf bases. The Venus flytrap has a trap that looks and smells like a flower to insects. When they land on it, they touch a trigger hair which slams the trap shut and they are then digested by the plant.

WHY DOES A COW CHEW ITS CUD?

Camels find this form of eating very useful for long desert journeys.

Many thousands of years ago, there were certain animals who couldn't protect themselves very well against their predators. In order to survive, these animals developed a special way of eating. They would snatch some food whenever they could, swallow it quickly without chewing, and run away to hide. When they were safe in their hiding place, they would chew the food at their leisure.

Some present day animals, such as cows, continue to eat in this way. It is called chewing the cud, and the animals are called ruminants. This way of eating is possible because such animals have complicated stomachs with five compartments. Each of these compartments processes the food.

WHEN IS THE BEST TIME TO SEE A BAT?

Bats are most easily spotted on open ground near ponds and rivers at dusk. Insects hatch and fly from the water in large numbers, which attracts the bats.

The bats catch the insects by a process known as echolocation. This is a technique in which an animal processes sounds and listens for the echoes reflected from surfaces and objects in the environment. From the information contained in these echoes, the animal is able to perceive the objects and work out exactly where they are. Bats change their roosting places from season to season. They choose caves, old ice houses and trees in which to hibernate. These give a constant temperature just above freezing.

THERE ARE MORE THAN 1,000 SPECIES OF BAT. OF THOSE, JUST THREE ARE VAMPIRE BATS, WHICH LIVE ON THE BLOOD OF OTHER ANIMALS.

• FACT FILE •

A bat called the pipistrelle has adapted to warm cavity walls or hanging tiles in our homes as their normal woodland habitat has been lost and natural roosts have become scarce.

WHEN DO HEDGEHOGS ROLL UP INTO A BALL?

Although hedgehogs like woodland scrub and cover, as their name suggests, they prefer well-cropped or cut grassland to find the worms and insects that are their staple diet.

Hedgehogs do not tunnel, but wrap themselves up in dense collections of leaves to form solid hibernation nests under cover. They hide breeding nests in similar places.

Hedgehogs roll themselves up into a ball with spines to protect themselves from most predators. The spines are erect when they roll up, and these form a sharp defence.

Hedgehogs are born with soft, white spines with dark spines soon growing in between. Fleas, ticks and lice enjoy life among these spines.

 DID YOU KNOW THAT HEDGEHOGS HAVE AROUND 5,000 SPINES? THEY ARE NOT RELATED TO ANY OTHER ANIMALS THAT HAVE SPINES.

FACT FILE

The porcupine is another mammal that uses its spines for defence. Porcupines are heavyset, relatively short-legged rodents, essentially nocturnal and herbivorous in habit.

WHERE ARE ELEPHANTS FOUND?

There are 40,000 muscles in an elephant's trunk.

Although elephants once seem to have inhabited many parts of the Earth, they are now found in their wild state only in Africa and tropical Asia. Thousands of years ago many kinds of giant monsters roamed about the Earth. Even though these beasts were immense in size, they were not able to endure the hardships they had to undergo, brought about by climate change and the disappearance of food. One by one they perished until there were only two species remaining, the African and Asiatic elephants.

Elephants are the largest land animals, and in many ways, among the most interesting. They are mild and gentle, reasonably intelligent and easier to train than most other animals.

• FACT FILE •

Mammoths were ancient relatives of elephants. Their skeletons can be seen in museums. Their bones have been discovered in caves and riverbeds in North America and Europe.

WHERE DID THE FIRST HORSE COME FROM?

Arabian horses

Horses evolved over millions of years, from far smaller animals in North America. During an ice age, when the sea level was lower than it is now, they spread west to Asia across the land bridge connecting Alaska and Siberia. From there, they spread as far as Europe, Arabia and Africa, evolving into different variations and even species, such as zebras, to suit their different environments. Species include the Tarpan of Eastern and southern Europe, the diminutive Shetland pony and Arab horses, renowned for their stamina and speed.

Humans have exploited horses for thousands of years and have selectively bred them to bring out particular characteristics. For example, all racehorses in the world are descended from Arab horses. The only truly wild species of horse alive today is the Przewalski's horse from Mongolia.

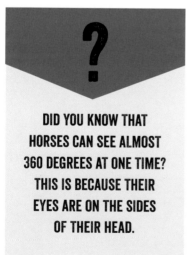

?

DID YOU KNOW THAT HORSES CAN SEE ALMOST 360 DEGREES AT ONE TIME? THIS IS BECAUSE THEIR EYES ARE ON THE SIDES OF THEIR HEAD.

FACT FILE

A zebra is a striped member of the horse family. There are three species of zebra – the common zebra, Grevy's zebra and the mountain zebra. They live in herds in the deserts and grasslands of eastern and southern Africa.

WHERE DID THE SPRINGBOK GET ITS NAME?

Springboks can survive up to ten years in the wild and live on a diet of grass, roots, leaves and flowers.

The springbok is small antelope that lives on the *veldt* (grassy plains) of southern Africa. *Bok* is the Afrikaans word for buck, and these pretty little animals are also called springbucks. Their main predators are lions and cheetahs, and if the springbok spot one of them, they distract the predator and warn the other members of the herd by leaping up to 2m (6½ft), more than double their own height, into the air, displaying the white flashes on their rumps, before dashing off. There used to be large herds of springbok in southern and southwestern Africa, but many were killed by huntsmen and farmers. They are members of the cattle family.

• FACT FILE •

Red deer are fascinating creatures to watch during the autumn rut. This is when the stags drive off rivals with roaring challenges, clashes of antlers and dramatic fights in order to secure a 'harem' of female deer (hinds).

WHERE IS A WOLF'S TERRITORY?

Wolves are among the largest members of the dog family and they live in communal groups called packs. Each pack has a territory that the wolves will not allow other wolves to enter. The size of the territory depends on how much prey is available: if food is scarce, a territory will be large, whereas if prey are plentiful, it can be small.

Packs are tightly knit groups, led by an alpha male and an alpha female, who are dominant over the other members. Often, only the alpha female will breed, in order to avoid there being too many cubs to feed.

Wolves are among the best cooperative hunters in the animal kingdom and their howls allow them to keep track of which member of the pack is where during a hunt. They typically hunt large mammals, such as deer, elk and caribou.

There are two main groups of wolves – grey wolves and red wolves. Red wolves tend to be smaller than grey wolves, but have longer legs.

FACT FILE

A wolf has excellent senses of vision, smell and hearing. These senses help the animal locate its prey. A wolf can see and smell a deer more than 1.6km (1 mile) away.

WHERE CAN YOU FIND A FOX'S DEN?

The common type of fox in Europe is the red fox. Contrary to popular thought, foxes are not members of the dog family. In the wild, foxes may dig their own burrow, take over a disused badger sett or nest in a hollow log. Urban foxes may nest under garden sheds or even under the floorboards of old houses. Usually the female fox (vixen) will only move to a den a short while before she is due to give birth.

Once the cubs are big enough to be left, she will find food for herself. After about five weeks she will start to bring small animals, such as rabbits and birds, for her cubs to eat. When they are strong enough, she will bring back live mice, frogs, rats or small birds so the cubs can practise hunting techniques.

• FACT FILE •

A female fox gives birth to her young in late winter or early spring. A young fox is called a cub. Red foxes have between 4 and 9 cubs in one litter. The male fox takes no part in bringing up the cubs.

WHAT IS A REPTILE?

Iguana

Lizard

A reptile is an air-breathing animal with a body structure comprising traits of amphibians, birds and mammals. Reptiles are generally scaly and their eggs are fertilized internally. Living reptiles include crocodiles, tortoises and turtles, snakes and lizards. There are about 6,000 surviving species. Long ago there were many more kinds of reptile, such as the dinosaurs and the flying pterosaurs. Most reptiles lay eggs or give birth to live young, which can then immediately live an independent existence.

FACT FILE

Tortoises and turtles are the only reptiles with shells. They pull their head, legs and tail into their shell, which serves as a suit of armour. Few other backboned animals have such excellent natural protection.

HOW DOES A CHAMELEON CHANGE ITS APPEARANCE?

The chameleon's appearance is controlled by body chemicals called hormones, which affect pigments in the skin.

The chameleon is a type of lizard. There are about 85 species and most of them live in the forests of Africa and Madagascar. Chameleons are known for their ability to change their appearance, but many other kinds of lizards also have this ability.

A chameleon may be green, yellow or white one minute, and the next it may be brown or black. Chameleons may also become spotted or blotched. Many people believe chameleons change to blend with their surroundings, but the changes actually occur in response to variations in light or temperature, or as the result of fright or some other reaction to their environment.

• FACT FILE •

Chameleons living in trees have a long, sticky tongue with which they capture their prey. The tongue, which may be as long as their entire body, is controlled by powerful muscles in the throat. The tongue shoots out so rapidly that the human eye can hardly see it.

HOW DO SNAKES MOVE?

Snakes have several ways of moving about. The most common way is for a snake to throw its body into loops and move forward by pressing against anything solid.

Another way in which a snake moves is by contracting its muscles, which pushes the body along rather like a concertina being squeezed open and shut.

The desert-living sidewinder moves by throwing a loop out to one side, then sliding its body towards the loop while throwing another loop sideways at the same time. The sidewinder looks like a spring rolling along the sand, but this is an effective way of moving on this soft surface. Most snakes are able to swim effectively by using a wriggling motion.

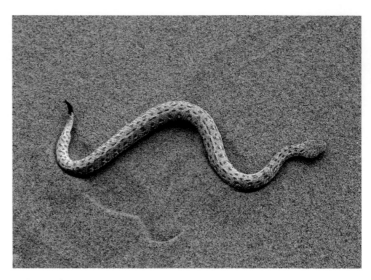
Sidewinder

JUST BECAUSE SNAKES DO NOT HAVE LEGS NOW, DOES NOT MEAN THEY DID NOT HAVE THEM AT SOME TIME IN THEIR DEVELOPMENT. SOME EXPERTS BELIEVE THAT THE ANCESTORS OF SNAKES WERE CERTAIN KINDS OF BURROWING LIZARDS.

HOW DO SNAKES INJECT THEIR POISON?

A venomous snake is one that has saliva glands that produce a substance that is poisonous to its prey. This substance is called the snake's venom. Some snakes' venom is so powerful it could kill an elephant. About two hundred venomous snakes (out of 412 species) can be considered dangerous to people.

Two of these are African snakes called the boomslang and the bird snake. Their fangs are in the rear of their mouths and are greatly enlarged and have grooves running down one side. Just above these fangs is an opening that leads to the venom-producing gland. When a rear-fanged snake bites, venom drips down the grooves into the wound made by the fangs. In cobras, however, the fangs are at the front of the mouth, one on each side of the upper jaw. A muscle surrounds the venom gland so that when the snake bites, the muscles press on the gland and force the venom down into the fang and out through the tip. The spitting cobra can spray venom from its fangs the way water is squirted from a toy gun.

WHY ARE CROCODILES NOT THE SAME AS ALLIGATORS?

Crocodile

Both crocodiles and alligators spend most of their lives in swamps and rivers in warm climates, although they breathe air through nostrils on the top of their snouts. They close these nostrils when they dive below the water. Caymans and gavials are relatives of crocodiles and alligators.

The simple way of telling them apart is that crocodiles show the fourth tooth in their lower jaw when their mouths are closed. Alligators, on the other hand, do not. It is probably wise not to go near enough to a live crocodile to find out, however, as they have been known to attack humans.

Alligator

FACT FILE

The Komodo dragon is a huge monitor lizard found living in Indonesia. This fearsome lizard is known to live for about 100 years. It can grow to a length of 3m (10ft).

WHY ARE SOME AMPHIBIANS POISONOUS?

Cane toad

Amphibians appeared approximately 370 million years ago and were the first-known vertebrates with four limbs.

Not all frogs are poisonous, but some have developed venom that they can use, should they come under attack from predators. The common toad contains a poison that it exudes through its skin if attacked. Dogs and cats commonly experience this poison, but seldom suffer serious effects. It does teach them, however, to avoid these amphibians.

Cane toads are very large toads that contain a drug capable of causing hallucinations if eaten. The skin of some frogs and toads contain poisons that are among the most powerful known to humans.

WHY DO
FROGS VANISH IN WINTER?

Frogs vary considerably in shape, colour and size. Some tree frogs that live in the USA are no more than 2.5cm (1in) in length. Leopard frogs are about 5–10cm (2–4in long) while bullfrogs can reach 20cm (8in) long with legs of 25cm (10in).

What do these frogs do in winter? In northern countries, when cold weather sets in, some frogs dive into a pond, bury themselves in the mud and stay there all winter. Ponds do not freeze solid, even when winters are very cold, so the frog does not freeze.

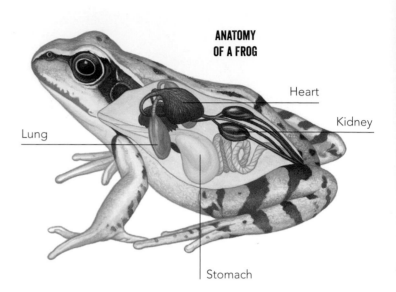

ANATOMY OF A FROG

Heart

Kidney

Lung

Stomach

The internal organs of a frog are typical of vertebrate animals, although their lungs and hearts are much simpler than those of mammals and birds.

HOW DO FROGS' EGGS HATCH?

Most amphibians lay their eggs in water. Frogs' eggs are called spawn. They are protected from predators by a thick layer of jelly. Inside this, a tadpole develops. When it hatches out, it is able to swim, using its long tail, and breathes through gills. As a tadpole grows, first hind legs and then fore legs begin to appear. Lungs develop, and the young frog is able to begin to breathe with its head above water. Gradually the tail shortens until the young frog resembles its adult parents.

Adult frogs often return to the pond in which they hatched.

Frog spawn hatches into larvae called tadpoles after about a week.

THE LIFE CYCLE OF AN AMPHIBIAN

At first tadpoles feed on algae and breathe through feathery gills.

By about ten weeks, the froglet has hind legs, internal gills and can eat small insects.

FACT FILE

The tree frog lives in the rainforests of South America and uses the pools of water in the centre of certain tropical plants. Although it can swim, it spends much of its life out of water, among the leaves of trees where there are plenty of insects for food. It has sticky toes that enable it to climb.

THE
BIRD WORLD

CONTENTS

HOW DO BIRDS FLY?

The bodies of birds are specially modified to give them the power of flight. Their bones are hollow to keep them light. Their bodies are also extremely lightweight, allowing them to glide and fly with the minimum of effort. For example, an eagle has a wingspan of more than 2m (6.5ft) and yet it weighs less than 4kg (9lb). Birds also have air sacs linked to their lungs to give them extra oxygen as they flap their wings.

However, flying is not just a matter of flapping wings up and down. It is a mixture of gliding and powered flight. When the wings are flapped they move in a complicated way, scooping air downwards and backwards. The wing actually twists so that the air is pushed back in the right direction to give lift. The wings are twisted again on the forward stroke so that they slide easily through the air without slowing down the bird's flight. A bird's feathers, which help to reduce wind resistance in flight, are ideal because they are very light, yet also strong and flexible.

A heron in flight

DID YOU KNOW THAT SOME BIRDS CANNOT FLY AT ALL? SUCH BIRDS INCLUDE PENGUINS, WHO USE THEIR WINGS IN WATER, ENABLING THEM TO SWIM VERY FAST.

• FACT FILE •

The falcon is a bird of prey that feeds on other birds and small animals. It is equipped with powerful talons and a sharp beak in order to kill and dismember its prey. When the falcon dives on its prey, it closes its enormous wings and drops like a stone to pick up speed. Powerful muscles in the bird's legs help to cushion the huge impact of the strike.

HOW DO BIRDS KNOW WHEN TO MIGRATE?

Man has been fascinated by the migration of birds since the very beginning of history. And yet we still don't have all the answers. By migration, we mean the movement of birds south in the autumn and north in the spring, or moving from lowlands to highlands, or from inland to the coast.

We know that some go to warmer climates because they cannot survive winter conditions. Also, those birds that feed on certain insects, or small rodents, wouldn't find any food in winter. Whatever the reason is, how do they actually know when to make this long flight? It is believed that birds can tell when the days get shorter (and longer in spring) and this acts as an 'alarm clock' to tell them that it is time to move along.

So it is the change in the length of the day and the disappearance of food that tell the bird to head to warmer places. There are many other factors involved, of course, and many things we still don't understand, but these are certainly the main reasons why birds migrate. The champions among birds that migrate are the Arctic terns. This amazing bird will travel as many as 35,410km (22,000 miles) during the course of a year, going back and forth!

• FACT FILE •

This map shows the migratory routes of some animals.

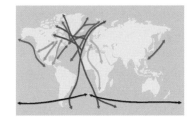

Blue whale ▮
Albatross ▮
Arctic tern ▮
Cuckoo ▮
Monarch butterfly ▮

WHAT DO BIRDS EAT?

• FACT FILE •

Bald eagles pluck fish out of the water with their talons, and sometimes follow seabirds as a means of locating fish. Besides live fish, bald eagles prey on other birds, small mammals, snakes, turtles and crabs.

Different species of bird have different diets, just as mammals do. Some are vegetarian, eating fruits and seeds. Others feed on insects and other invertebrates, such as worms. Birds' beaks are adapted to the kind of food they need. The beaks of meat-eaters are often hooked and sharp, ideal for tearing flesh from carcasses. Birds that search for food along the seashore or on mud banks often have long pointed beaks for burrowing into soft ground. It is fascinating to watch seabirds dive into the water. Gannets, for example, plunge in very spectacularly, head-first with folded wings, from up to 30m (98ft) or in a lower slanting dive. They disappear deep underwater, often with a splash of spray. Another bird to watch feeding is the swift or martin. These are all insect-eaters and feed on the wing. They can be seen circling above water to catch their prey.

WHY IS A BIRD'S VISION SO GOOD?

A BIRD'S EYE TAKES UP ABOUT 50 PER CENT OF ITS HEAD, WHILE A HUMAN EYE TAKES UP ABOUT 5 PER CENT OF THE HEAD. A HUMAN'S EYES WOULD NEED TO BE THE SIZE OF BASEBALLS TO BE COMPARABLE.

Vision is the dominant sense of nearly all birds. In most, the eyes are placed so far to the side of the head that they have mainly monocular vision, meaning that each eye scans a separate area. This feature is shared by all hunted creatures who depend on vision to warn them of possible danger. Birds of prey and owls have eyes set more to the front of the head, offering a wider angle of binocular vision, which is vitally important for judging distance. Birds also have a third eyelid, which moves sideways across the cornea and keeps it moist without interrupting their vision.

FACT FILE

Accuracy is crucial for hunting birds like eagles, which rely on their keen eyesight, first to spot the prey and then to catch it.

Eagles' eyes are therefore positioned sufficiently far forward to give them binocular or three-dimensional vision.

WHAT ARE FEATHERS MADE OF?

Feathers consist of beta keratin, which is a form of protein, and are considered to have evolved from reptilian scales. Keratin can also be found in hair, hoofs and fingernails.

Contour feathers are periodically moulted, and other keratinized structures such as the bill and claws may be moulted as well.

Specialized nerve endings are present throughout the skin of birds. There is a preen gland, which is located on the back – just in front of the tail – and secretes oil for grooming the feathers. This gland is most pronounced in aquatic birds, to ensure that their feathers are waterproof.

The many different types of feather are designed for insulation, flight, formation of body contours, display and sensory reception. Unlike the hair of most mammals, feathers do not cover the entire skin surface of birds but are arranged in symmetrical tracts with areas of bare skin.

Adult birds grow new feathers at least once a year. For a song-bird, such as a thrush, this could take 5 to 12 weeks, while for a bird of prey it might take several years.

• FACT FILE •

Penguins have feathers but they cannot fly. They can swim at great speed using their wings as flippers to power them in the water.

WHERE WOULD YOU SEE A CONTOUR FEATHER?

A feather is one of the light, thin growths that cover a bird's body. Birds can have two main kinds of feather – contour and down.

Contour feathers grow on a bird's body in tracts, or lines, called pterylae. From the pterylae, the relatively large contour feathers fan out to cover the bird almost completely. Down feathers are found on all parts of a bird's body.

Unlike hair and scales, feathers have a complicated branching pattern. Feathers enable a bird to fly and help it maintain a constant body temperature. Although feathers are remarkably durable, they gradually wear out. Birds shed their feathers and grow a new set at least once a year. This process is called moulting.

 A HUMMINGBIRD HAS AROUND 1,000 FEATHERS, WHILE SWANS HAVE AS MANY AS 25,000.

FACT FILE

People have used feathers for a variety of purposes. For hundreds of years American Indians used feathers to make arrows and headdresses. Until the mid-19th century, when pens with steel nibs became popular, most people wrote with quill pens. Today, manufacturers use feathers as stuffing in pillows and upholstery.

WHY DOES THE PEACOCK RAISE HIS FEATHERS?

The common peacock originates from India, but has been known in the West for thousands of years. The long train, which is not actually a tail, but is held up by the feathers of true tail beneath, is about half the total length of the male bird.

Only the males have trains; the females – peahens – are smaller, drab in colour and have smaller crests.

The male uses his beautiful plumage to impress females and in the breeding season will raise and quiver his train feathers in order to persuade them that he would make a good father for their chicks. Males are often used as living garden ornaments in grand gardens and public parks.

Some peacocks and peahens are pure white. This is a colour mutation and, in captivity, selective breeding has been employed to produce this colour variation.

Peacock feathers have long been used in decorating hats, but in many areas it is thought bad luck to have them in the house.

• FACT FILE •

Ostriches lay bigger eggs than any other bird – they are 24 times bigger than a chicken's egg. The shell is so strong that even if you stand on top of an ostrich egg, it will not break. An ostrich's eyes are nearly as big as tennis balls!

?

DID YOU KNOW THAT THE COMMON PEACOCK IS THE NATIONAL BIRD OF INDIA? IT IS ALSO SACRED IN THE HINDU RELIGION, BECAUSE THE SPOTS ON ITS TAIL REPRESENTS THE EYES OF THE HINDU GODS.

WHY IS A MALE BIRD BRIGHTER THAN A FEMALE?

Female birds choose a mate based on how attractive they find him!

In many, but not all, bird species, the male has brighter plumage than the female and uses it to attract the female's attention and to see off rival males. Some birds also sing for the same purposes.

The female birds of most species do not need to display and are thought to have duller plumage because it makes it harder for predators to find them when they are sitting on the nest.

Not all birds keep their bright plumage all year round: male mallard ducks lose their bright green head feathers and their striking wing patterns after the breeding season. In puffins, the beak changes: after the breeding season, they lose the bright-coloured outer parts of the beak and regrow them for the following spring.

• FACT FILE •

The puffin's big, bright beak is hinged so that it can snap up fish and still keep a grip on those it has already caught.

WHEN DOES A CYGNET BECOME A SWAN?

A male swan is called a cob, and a female swan is called a pen.

Young swans, or cygnets, are hatched with a complete covering of down and can take to the water as soon as they leave the nest, within 24 to 48 hours. Right from the beginning they can forage for themselves, but at least one parent remains with them, guarding, guiding and, initially, brooding them at night. The dark downy plumage is retained for two to six weeks and is then replaced gradually by the juvenile feathers. The flight feathers are the last to develop, taking from five weeks to as many months. By the age of six months the cygnets are practically indistinguishable from adults, both in plumage and in size.

• FACT FILE •

In captivity geese and swans have been known to live for more than 30 years; there are reports of geese exceeding 40 years of age. With luck and cunning a wild swan may survive for 15 to 20 years.

WHEN IS THE BEST TIME TO SEE AN OWL?

• FACT FILE •

Some owls are helpful to farmers because they destroy rats, insects and other enemies of crops. But there are owls that are fond of chickens and other domestic fowl, and these owls cost the farmer a lot of money.

Owls are thick-set, rounded birds with large, flat or rounded heads and legs. An owl is difficult to see because it really comes to life at night, and its whole body is especially suited to this kind of life. Once the owl has startled its prey and heard its movement, it can even see it in the dark. This is because the eyeballs of the owl are elastic. It can focus them instantly for any distance. The owl can also open the pupil of its eye very wide. This enables it to make use of all the night light there is. An owl's eyes are placed so that it has to turn its whole head to change the direction of its glance. Even the owl's feathers help it to hunt for its food. The feathers are so soft that the owl can fly noiselessly and thus swoop right down onto its prey.

WHEN DO WOODPECKERS PECK WOOD?

There are few birds that are as specialized as the woodpecker. They are rarely seen away from the trees that they need to supply their food and nest sites. They are particularly noted for their probing for insects in tree bark and chiselling nest holes in dead wood.

Most woodpeckers spend their entire lives in trees spiralling up the tree trunks in search of insects. In the spring you can hear the loud calls of woodpeckers, often accompanied by drumming on hollow wood or occasionally on metal. These are the sounds that are associated with the males marking their territories. Most woodpeckers tend to be rather solitary or travel in pairs.

The green woodpecker's tongue is long and sticky, with a barbed point. It probes into anthills and the ants are dragged out and swallowed. When not being used, the tongue winds back, liked a coiled spring, into a groove under the top of the woodpecker's skull.

Hairy woodpecker

Green woodpecker

FACT FILE

Most woodpeckers eat insects, but some feed on fruits and berries, and sapsuckers regularly feed on sap from certain trees in some seasons.

WHERE WOULD A COCKATOO BE A PEST?

Sulphur-crested cockatoo

Cockatoos are large members of the parrot family that are native to Australia and New Guinea. There are several species, which may be a mix of white, grey, black, rose-pink or red, but the best known is the sulphur-crested cockatoo. Like all cockatoos, they have a large crest on their heads that they can raise and lower. They are strong birds and use their beaks to help them to climb. In fruit- and nut-growing areas of Australia they can pose problems for farmers because they feed in large flocks and can ruin a vast area of an orchard in just minutes.

They are clever birds, and can be trained to talk. Their usual call is a loud, raucous screech, which can be heard ringing through eucalypt forests and public parks and gardens across much of eastern and northern Australia.

• FACT FILE •

Many species of parrot are prized for their ability to repeat words or to learn complicated tricks. The famous pirate Long John Silver, from the story *Treasure Island*, was renowned for having a talking parrot on his shoulder.

Macaws

HOW DOES THE
KING PENGUIN PROTECT ITS EGGS?

A king penguin

King penguins do not build nests, but tuck their single egg under their bellies while resting it on their feet, protected by a large fold of skin. Mother and father penguin take turns keeping the egg warm in the cold.

Because the king penguin's main concern seems to be maintaining a constant body temperature, they are limited to places that do not have temperature fluctuations. Their territories can be rocky, icy or snowy, as long as there is water and an abundance of food.

Colonies can be as large as 10,000 penguins, and each bird keeps its distance from the others. In these confined spaces, coming too close earns a nasty jab or flipper slap! The king penguin, second in size only to the huge emperor penguin, is one of the biggest birds and grows up to 90cm (3ft). They can swim at speeds of 6mph (9km/h), and use their wings as flippers to fly through the water, and then hop out onto the rocky shore. Unlike many other penguins, the king penguin runs and doesn't hop while on land.

FACT FILE

Baby chicks are born from their greenish-white eggs nearly naked, but quickly grow a brown woolly fuzz to keep them warm. The adult penguins are often dwarfed by their chicks.

King penguins sometimes dive as deep as 275m (900ft) to look for food, and can stay submerged for as long as five minutes.

WHERE WOULD YOU SEE A PUFFIN?

You are likely to see puffins only in early summer on high clifftops in remote coastal areas and islands of the British Isles and on the Atlantic coast of Norway, Sweden and Finland.

Hugh colonies of puffins nest in burrows in early summer and each pair raises a single chick. During the breeding season both male and female develop the large, brightly coloured beak. In winter they stay far out at sea.

Rises in sea temperature because of global warming and overfishing have reduced the stocks of their typical food – the sand eel – so numbers of puffins are also dropping.

FACT FILE

Although puffins are ungainly while on the ground and their short wings mean that they are not very agile fliers, they are supremely adapted for swimming underwater, where they catch sand eels.

?

DID YOU KNOW THAT PUFFINS ARE SOMETIMES CALLED 'SEA PARROTS' OR 'CLOWNS OF THE SEA'?

WHY DO BIRDS SING?

Male birds sing for two reasons: to attract mates in the breeding season, and to warn other males to keep out of their territory.

Birds also use other calls to communicate with one another. When flying together, geese call to make sure that they stay in touch and adult penguins can recognize the voice of their own chick from among thousands in a colony.

Birds know instinctively how to sing, but some species can learn to add new notes to their songs. Birds that are good at imitation, like starlings, incorporate the sounds of car alarms in their songs and, in Australia, some superb lyrebirds have learned to imitate the noise of a chainsaw.

FACT FILE

If danger threatens her chicks, a hen will make a quiet noise that warns them to be still so that they do not attract attention.

NEARLY HALF OF THE WORLD'S BIRDS ARE SONGBIRDS – THERE ARE AROUND 4,000 SPECIES, DIVIDED INTO 35 TO 55 FAMILIES.

WHICH BIRDS CAN TALK BEST?

Not all parrots can talk. African grey parrots are more likely to talk than others.

Several families of birds can be trained to 'talk'. In reality they are simply mimicking noises without really understanding what they are saying, although they can be taught to associate a given word or phrase with a particular action – for example, saying 'give us a peanut' to get a reward. The best talkers are parrots and mynas, and members of the crow family such as crows, jackdaws and ravens can also learn a few simple words. They can do this because they are highly intelligent birds and they are excellent mimics in the wild. Other bird mimics are starlings and some of the bowerbirds in Australia, including one individual that learned to copy the noise of the logging machines that were destroying his habitat.

HOW DOES A PIGEON FIND ITS WAY HOME?

Homing pigeons are well known for their ability to find their way back to their roost, and racing pigeons can fly as many as 800km (500 miles) in a day to do so. No one is entirely sure how they do this: some scientists think they have an organ within their brains that reads changes in the Earth's magnetic field. When they are close to their home, they also appear to navigate by following landmarks that they have learned to recognize, such as roads and rivers.

Some birds that migrate long distances, such as swifts and common terns, seem to be born knowing where to fly as the young have to make their own way. Migrating geese, swans and starlings travel in family groups so that the adults can lead the young in the correct direction.

FACT FILE

Homing pigeons have been used to carry messages for more than 3,000 years, including during both World Wars I and II. The Dickin Medal – known as the animal Victoria Cross – was awarded to 32 pigeons that flew information across the English channel during World War II.

HOW DID THE GOLDEN EAGLE GET ITS NAME?

The golden eagle is North America's largest predatory bird. The plumage of an adult eagle is mainly brown, darkening towards the wings, while the tail is greyish-brown. The feathers at the head and nape of its neck are golden brown, hence its name.

The golden eagle is a supreme flier. Using the rising air on the sides of their mountain habitat, they rise and spiral high into the air, covering vast areas of ground. They can ride air currents between ridges, and glide down at speeds of up to 190km/h (120mph), then swoop up gracefully to their next landing point. This bird's flight is very graceful when moving slowly in still air, or even when battling against near hurricane force headwinds. Occasionally, they dive vertically onto their prey, and at times their speed is said to rival that of the fastest falcons.

? DID YOU KNOW THAT EAGLES FEATURE ON THE COATS OF ARMS OF MANY COUNTRIES, INCLUDING MEXICO, EGYPT, POLAND, GERMANY AND AUSTRIA.

FACT FILE

The buzzard is quite common in many areas of Britain, and often perches on wires or telegraph poles, something an eagle would never do. Sometimes, a buzzard can also be seen circling above its nesting territories.

WHAT ARE CURLEWS AND GODWITS?

Curlews and godwits are both long-billed wading birds. The curlew is related to the sandpiper and the snipe. It is found throughout the Americas, from Patagonia, in the far south of South America, to the Arctic in North America. It also lives in Europe and Asia. Curlews have long, slender bills that curve downward. Although they are wading birds, they nest on dry ground, often far from water. The name derives from the curlew's slender bill, which it uses to catch small crabs, shellfish, snails, worms and beetles.

A godwit's bill curves slightly upward. These birds have greyish or brownish feathers marked with spots and streaks. Godwits nest in marshes or grassy areas in northern Europe, Canada and the northern part of the United States.

Black-tailed godwit

Curlew

FACT FILE

An avocet is another wading bird with a long, curved bill. The avocet feeds by scraping its bill along the bottom of shallow pools of water. In this way it collects small water animals, which it eats. It also eats other food that floats on or in the water.

HOW DOES A KINGFISHER CATCH ITS FOOD?

The kingfisher is the name of a large family of birds found all over the world; they have large heads and long, heavy, pointed bills, short legs and short stubby tails. Their outer and middle toes are joined together by strong membranes.

The kingfisher may spend long hours sitting on a branch beside a lake or stream watching for the small fish that swim near the surface. Then, sometimes hovering for a moment in midair, the bird dives after a fish. Kingfishers usually seize their food, but occasionally they spear fish with their long bills. They then toss the fish into the air, catch it and swallow it headfirst. Kingfishers also eat crayfish, frogs, tadpoles, salamanders and insects.

• FACT FILE •

Kingfishers burrow in the steep walls of riverbanks or sandbanks. They dig a tunnel from 1.2 to 4.6m (4 to 15 ft) long with a larger hollow at the end where they build a nest of fish bones and scales.

RIVER
AND SEA LIFE

CONTENTS

HOW MANY KINDS OF FISH ARE THERE?

Fish, like all creatures that existed thousands of years ago, have undergone many changes in their development. There were fish in the oceans before humans ever appeared on the Earth. In the world today there are more living species of fish than of any other class of backboned animals. There are around 40,000 different kinds of fish living in every kind of water from mountain torrents and tiny ponds to the depths of the Earth's oceans.

Fish are divided into three general types: the cartilaginous fish, which includes sharks, skate and rays. The second type is the bony fish, which has a complete bony skeleton and is covered with bony scales. This group of fish is the most common and accounts for over 90 per cent of all fish. Finally there are lungfish, a special type of fish with two sets of breathing equipment, possessing both gills and lungs.

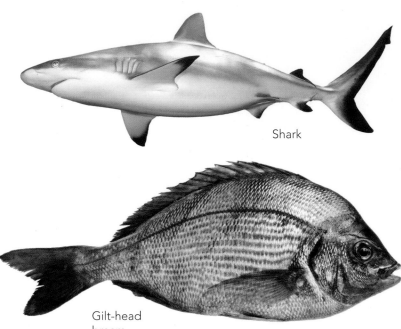

Shark

Gilt-head bream

HOW CAN FISH BREATHE UNDERWATER?

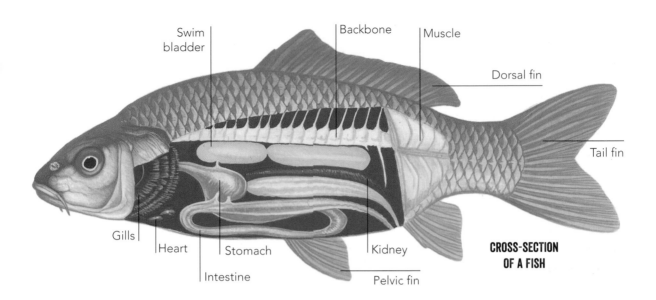

Swim bladder   Backbone   Muscle

Dorsal fin

Tail fin

Gills

Heart   Stomach   Kidney

Intestine   Pelvic fin

CROSS-SECTION OF A FISH

Fish are able to breath underwater because they have special organs called gills. Gills are bars of tissue at the side of a fish's head. They have masses of finger-like projections that contain tiny blood vessels. Water goes into the fish's mouth and flows over its gills. The gill filaments take in oxygen (which is dissolved) from the water and pass it into the fish's blood.

In this way the gills have the same function as the lungs of air-breathing animals. If water is contaminated, fish need to take oxygen from another source. Some attempt to come to the surface of the water and take in oxygen from the air. However, their gills are neither suitable nor adept at processing oxygen from the air.

Fish are able to smell, although they do not use their gills for this. They have two small nostrils on their heads which act as organs of smell. The sense of smell is much more developed in some fish than it is in others. Sharks, for example, rely on their keen sense of smell to hunt down and catch other animals to feed on.

• FACT FILE •

Cleaner fish are tiny creatures living in coral reefs. They regularly clean parasites from much larger fish. Even large predatory fish queue up to be cleaned of skin parasites. The cleaner fish swims into the predators's mouth without any risk of being eaten.

CAN FISH SEE IN THE DARK?

Fish tend to have the best possible eyesight for the zones in which they live. Most fish can see in colour.

Fish cannot see in total darkness, but their other senses help them to find food. Some, such as the anglerfish, actually carry their own lights.

Oceans offer various habitats at different depths below the surface. These are called zones. The euphotic zone is at the top, extending to a depth of about 200m (660ft). Very little light from the Sun can reach further down than this. The bathypelagic zone below is totally dark, so no plants can live there, but a number of fish, squid and crustaceans make this zone their home. They feed on waste material that sinks from above.

WHERE WOULD YOU SEE A SWORDFISH?

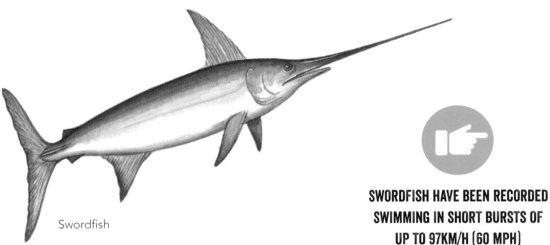

Swordfish

SWORDFISH HAVE BEEN RECORDED SWIMMING IN SHORT BURSTS OF UP TO 97KM/H (60 MPH)

Swordfish live in tropical and temperate seas, where they feed on fish and, sometimes, squid. They get their name from the elongated upper jaw, on which they spike their prey before juggling it into their mouths and swallowing it whole. They use their speed to catch up with their prey and so need to be able to move very fast through the water. Like some other fish, such as sharks, they have no scales to reduce drag. Like some sharks, too, the females hatch their eggs within their bodies rather than laying eggs, which means that the young are larger before they have to face any predators.

In places like Florida, swordfish are a popular sportfish: because they are so large and so strong, it can take a long time to tire them out so that they can be landed, so fishermen regard them as a real challenge.

• FACT FILE •

Most of a fish's body is composed of powerful muscles and its internal organs are squeezed into a tiny area. The fins are used to propel and stabilize the fish in the water.

WHY DO SALMON GO UPSTREAM TO SPAWN?

Salmon have a natural instinct to return to the place they were born to lay their eggs (to spawn). This is a safe place, usually a quiet area of a river, where young salmon can grow. The adult salmon have fed at sea but stop eating when they reach fresh water, so most die of exhaustion after spawning.

The eggs hatch after about two months, the young salmon stay near the hatchery for a few months, or even years, depending on the species, then make the journey down river to the sea. They will stay far out at sea for up to four years, before returning to the same river to breed.

AN ADULT SALMON HAS BEEN KNOWN TO COVER OVER 3,200KM (20,000 MILES) TO REACH THEIR SPAWNING GROUND!

WHAT IS A CRUSTACEAN?

Crustaceans are aquatic arthropods such as crabs, lobsters and shrimps. They have very tough, jointed external skeletons and jointed walking legs. Their bodies are divided into a region that contains most of the internal organs, covered by a shell called the carapace, and a muscular tail section that is usually folded under the body. Many crustaceans have powerful pincers that they use to capture and break up their prey, and to signal to others of their species. Crustaceans live in the sea and also freshwater habitats. Many small crustaceans feed on plankton. These crustaceans then are eaten by larger fish, and even whales. Crustaceans thus form an important link between the small food-producing organisms and the larger animals in the aquatic food chain.

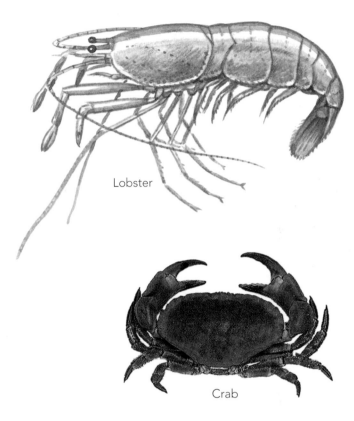

Lobster

Crab

WHAT ARE MUSSELS?

Mussels are molluscs and are related to water snails. Because their shells are divided into two halves, they are called bivalves.

The shell protects the soft body of the animal. A powerful foot enables the animal to change its position. Mussels suck in water and extract the oxygen and food that they require.

Marine and freshwater mussels can be found worldwide. Marine mussels prefer cool seas. Freshwater mussels, also known as naiads, inhabit streams, lakes and ponds and there are around 1,000 known species.

Mussel shells are dark blue or dark greenish brown on the outside, while on the inside they have a pearly appearance.

Swan mussel

Mussels attach themselves to solid objects or to one another by strands called byssus threads and often appear in dense clusters.

HOW DANGEROUS ARE JELLYFISH?

Not all jellyfish are dangerous, but many can cause severe pain and the stings of several can be fatal without rapid treatment. Among the most dangerous is the box jellyfish that lives in vast swarms in the southern oceans.

The body of most jellyfish is shaped like an upturned bowl, and has a thick layer of a jellylike substance between two layers of body cells. The dangerous part of the jellyfish is the long stinging tentacles. When the stinging cells come into contact with prey, they inject poison into it to paralyze or kill it. Jellyfish eat fish, plankton and smaller jellyfish.

The Portuguese man-of-war, which drifts on the surface of warm oceans around the world is not a true jellyfish, but a colony of modified jellyfish and other creatures with specialist functions such as capturing and digesting food. The blue 'head' is one member of the colony which has become a float filled with gas. The members of the colony share a common digestive system.

Portuguese
man-of-war

FACT FILE

The octopus belongs to a group of animals called 'cephalopods', which means they are 'head-footed' because the foot is divided into long arm-like tentacles that grow out from the head. An octopus has eight such tentacles.

IS IT TRUE MALE SEAHORSES BECOME MOTHERS?

The seahorse is a small fish that is so named because its head resembles that of a tiny horse. We are accustomed to the idea that it is always the female that bears the offspring, but in seahorses it is the reverse. The female seahorse, when she lays her eggs, puts them into a pouch beneath the tail of the male.

When the young have hatched and are ready to leave the pouch, the mouth of the pouch opens wide. The male alternately bends and straightens his body in convulsive jerks and a baby seahorse is shot out. After each birth the male rests, and when all the babies are born he shows signs of extreme exhaustion.

?

DID YOU KNOW THAT THERE ARE 53 SPECIES OF SEAHORSE? THEY RANGE IN SIZE FROM LESS THAN 2.5CM (1IN) TO 35.5CM (14IN) LONG.

• FACT FILE •

The seahorse has been described as having the head of a horse, the tail of a monkey, the pouch of a kangaroo, the hard outer skeleton of an insect and the independently moving eyes of a chameleon.

HOW DO STARFISH SEE?

Starfish do not have eyes as we think of them but at the end of each arm is a light-sensitive red eye spot surrounded by a circle of spines. Starfish do not see colour but can detect if, for instance, something dark is moving in front of a pale background. They frequently raise the tips of their arms to spot their prey. They also have a tiny tentacle at the end of each arm that can detect chemical changes and vibrations in the water.

Many starfish eat molluscs, which they pull apart with their suckered arms. Then they push their stomach out through their mouth and injest the mollusc.

The crown of thorns starfish eats coral, and has caused serious damage to the Great Barrier Reef off the coast of Australia.

THERE ARE AROUND 2,000 SPECIES OF STARFISH IN THE WORLD.

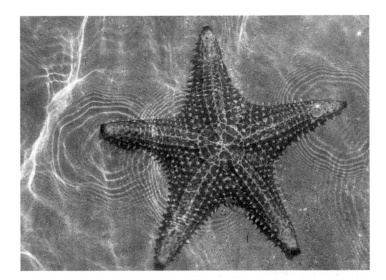

• FACT FILE •

Coelenterata are a group of small animals including sea anemones, jellyfish and corals. Most of them live in the sea and have arms covered with stinging cells. They feed on plankton.

WHAT DOES AN OCTOPUS EAT?

There are more than 150 species of octopus, ranging from the very small to the giant octopus, which can reach 10m (33ft) in length. Most of them eat crabs, fish, crustaceans and smaller molluscs, which they catch and tear apart with their suckered tentacles. An octopus' mouth is shaped like a parrot's beak, with two very strong jaws. In addition the octopus can inject venom or poison with its bite, enabling it to disable prey that might fight back, such as crabs, more quickly. Octopuses are very intelligent, curious animals, with a highly developed nervous system and extremely good eyesight. They propel themselves through the ocean by squirting water from the edge of their mantle. They are opportunistic feeders, which means that they will tackle almost anything when they are hungry!

• FACT FILE •

The Portuguese man-of-war's tentacles contain a very dangerous toxin that can be fatal to humans in large doses. This sea creature can grow up to 20m (66ft) in length.

WHEN DO WHITE SEALS TURN DARK?

The common seal can be found on sandy estuaries, fjords and rocky inlets away from the full force of the open sea. Although they live and feed in the water, they still come to the shore to breed and to moult their hair. A seal pup is born with thick white fur but will lose this shortly after it is born and it will be replaced by a much darker, sleeker coat. Their diet includes all kinds of seafoods: fish, shellfish, crabs and lobsters.

• FACT FILE •

The pup of a seal will suckle for ten minutes, five or six times a day. Its birth weight doubles in one week. After one month of rapid growth, the mother leaves to mate with another bull. The pup enters the sea to fend for itself.

Seals live in most of the world's oceans, but mainly in the Arctic and Antarctic. Some seals inhabit areas of the tropics.

WHERE IS A CLAM'S FOOT?

Clams are a type of mollusc, a group of soft-bodied animals that have no bones. They use a large, muscular organ called a foot to burrow in mud or sand. The foot spreads beneath the body, and its muscles move in a rippling motion that makes the animal move forward. A clam is an animal whose soft body is covered with a protective shell. They also have a heart, blood vessels and kidneys. Clams live on the bottom or along the shores of oceans, lakes and streams in many parts of the world. They feed on tiny water organisms called plankton, or on small, shrimp-like animals.

?

DID YOU KNOW THAT CLAMS HAVE NO SENSES? THEY CANNOT SMELL, HEAR OR EVEN SEE, BECAUSE THEY HAVE NO NOSE, EARS OR EYES.

• FACT FILE •

The giant clam lives on coral reefs in the Red Sea, the Indian Ocean and the Western Pacific. These clams can grow to a length of more than 1.2 m (4 ft).

HOW DO
WHALES BREATHE?

A baleen whale has two blowholes in the top of its head, while the toothed whale only has a single one. The 'blow' is caused by condensation from the warm, moist air that is exhaled, not from seawater trapped in the blowhole, as was once believed.

Whales take in air less frequently than land mammals, and they can hold their breath for extraordinarily long periods during their dives. Although their lung capacity is no greater than that of land mammals of equivalent size, whales take deeper breaths and extract more oxygen from the air they breathe. Unlike the seal, which exhales before diving, a whale's lungs are still partially inflated.

The whale's nostrils are modified to form a blowhole at the top of the head. The skin immediately surrounding the blowhole has many specialized nerve endings, which are very sensitive to the change as the blowhole breaks the water. The whale often breathes in and out again very rapidly, in the fraction of a second that the blowhole is above the surface. The blowhole is closed when the animal is submerged. When a whale surfaces and exhales, a spout of water or 'blow' can be seen.

BLUE WHALES ARE THE LARGEST CREATURES ON EARTH, YET THEY EAT SOME OF THE SMALLEST. AN ADULT CAN CONSUME AROUND 3 TONNES (3.3 TONS) OF SHRIMPLIKE KRILL A DAY!

MINIBEASTS

CONTENTS

WHAT ARE ARTHROPODS?

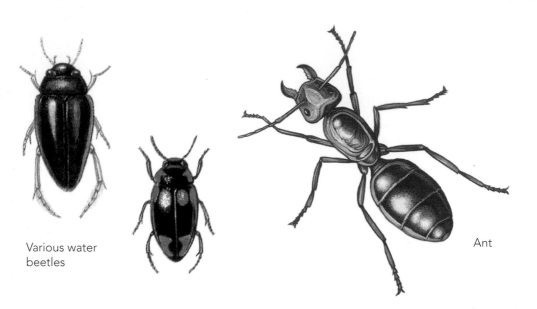

Various water beetles

Ant

Arthropods are animals with a hard external skeleton like a suit of armour. The skeleton is jointed to allow movement. Arthropods have evolved in a different way to vertebrates and even their blood is chemically different and so it is not red. They do not have a brain and spinal cord like vertebrates. Instead, they have a nerve cord running along the underside of their body, and small thickenings of this nerve cord instead of a brain. Arthropods have efficient eyes, but these work in a different way from those of vertebrates. Arthropods such as spiders may have many eyes.

• FACT FILE •

The most important groups of arthropods are the following: insects; crustaceans (including this red-banded sea shrimp); arachnids; chilopods or centipedes; and diplopods or millipedes.

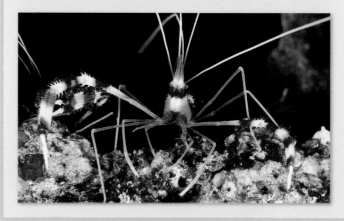

WHY ARE SPIDERS NOT INSECTS?

Spiders are meat-eaters. They feed on insects and other spiders that become trapped in their webs.

Spiders belong to the class of arachnids, which also includes scorpions, ticks and mites. None of these are actually classed as insects. Unlike insects, they have eight legs, eight eyes in most cases, no wings and only two, not three parts to their bodies.

Spiders are found in practically every kind of climate. They can run on the ground, climb plants, run on water and some even live in water.

The spider manufactures a silk in certain glands found in the abdomen or belly and uses this to spin its web. At the tip of the abdomen there are spinning organs that contain many tiny holes. The silk is forced through these tiny holes. When the silk comes out it is a liquid. As soon as it comes into contact with the air, it becomes solid.

• FACT FILE •

The scorpion is related to the spider. A scorpion has four pairs of walking legs and a pair of strong pincers, which it uses to grasp its prey. It also has a long, thin, jointed tail that ends in a curved, pointed stinger. This stinger is connected to poison glands.

WHEN DO BEES MAKE HONEY?

Bees constantly make honey because it serves them as food. So the whole process of making honey is a way of storing up food for the bee colony. The first thing a bee does is visit flowers and drink the nectar. Then it carries the nectar home in the honey sac. This is a bag-like enlargement of the digestive tract just in front of the bee's stomach.

The first step in making the honey takes place while the nectar is in the bee's honey sac. The sugars found in the nectar undergo a chemical change. The next step is to remove a large part of the water from the nectar. This is done by evaporation, which takes place because of the heat of the hive, and by ventilation. Honey stored in the honeycombs by honeybees has so much water removed from the original nectar that it will keep almost forever!

The honey is put into honeycombs to ripen, and to serve as the future food supply for the colony. Honeys differ in taste and appearance, depending on the source of the nectar.

• FACT FILE •

Honey is removed from the hive by various methods. It may be squeezed from the comb by presses, or it may be sold in the combs cut from the hive. Most honey, however, is removed from the combs by a machine known as a 'honey extractor'.

WHERE DO BEES GO IN WINTER?

Red-tailed bumblebee

White-tailed bumblebee

What happens to the bees in a colony depends on the kind of bees they are and where in the world they live. For bumblebees, which live in small colonies, only the young queens born in the summer will survive the winter, in a burrow in sandy ground or an abandoned mouse hole. In a honeybee colony, many of the bees will die, but many will live on, feeding on the honey that they have stored during the summer. The exceptions are the drones, who will be driven from the hive as the weather gets cooler because they are not needed during the winter. It is vital that the temperature in the hive does not drop too low, so during the autumn the workers will draughtproof it with a hard amber-coloured substance called propylis and in winter they will use muscle spasms to raise their body heat and thus keep the temperature of the hive at at least 7.2°C (45°F). On warm winter days (when the temperature is above 12°C (53.6°F), they may fly, hunting for nectar from the few flowers that are out, and will clear out rubbish from the floor of the hive.

FACT FILE

A typical honeybee colony is made up of one queen, tens of thousands of workers, and a few hundred drones. The queen is the female honeybee which lays eggs. The workers are the sterile female offspring of the queen. The drones are the male offspring.

WHERE DOES SILK COME FROM?

Thousands of years ago China had learned the secret of making silk cloth from the fine web spun by the silkworm, when it makes its cocoon. This secret was jealously guarded, and anyone who carried silkworms or their eggs out of China was punished by death.

Today silkworms are raised in China, Japan, India, France, Spain and Italy. The best silk is produced by the caterpillar of a small white moth, which feeds on the leaves of the white mulberry. In the early summer each female moth lays around 500 eggs. After the eggs have hatched into tiny black worms, they start to move their heads slowly back and forth. This means they are ready to spin their cocoons. The cocoon, which may contain as much as 457–1,097m (500–1,200yd) of thread, is finished in about 72 hours.

• FACT FILE •

The chief substance of most cocoons is silk. But the larva often incorporates other substances, including soil, sand grains, plant materials and hair or waste from its own body.

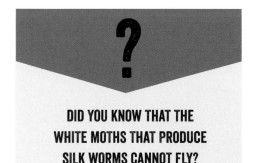

?

DID YOU KNOW THAT THE WHITE MOTHS THAT PRODUCE SILK WORMS CANNOT FLY?

WHEN DO GLOW-WORMS GLOW?

The glow-worm is not really a worm at all. It is a firefly in an early stage of development, called the larval stage. Most adult fireflies never eat because they did all their eating when they were larvae. They hide during the daytime among the vegetation. After dark, the female climbs up plant stems and the top of her abdomen glows. The light attracts tiny flies and mosquitoes for the larva to eat.

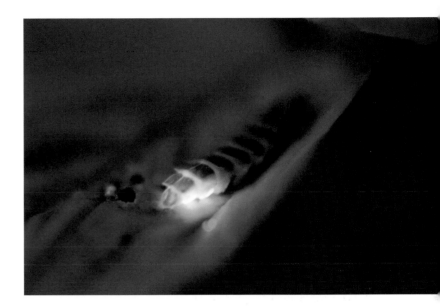

The Waitomo Caves in New Zealand house a memorable type of glow-worm. Tourists entering the Glowworm Caves in small boats see thousands of lights on the cave ceiling. The glow-worms look like stars in a night sky. If you cough or use a camera flash, the lights instantly go off. But wait quietly for a few minutes and they flicker back on, until the cave-ceiling 'sky' is again filled with 'stars'.

DID YOU KNOW THAT GLOW-WORMS ARE CARNIVORES? THEY EAT SNAILS, SLUGS AND INSECTS.

• FACT FILE •

Woodworm, the larvae of the furniture beetle, cause lots of damage to timber both in buildings and in the wild. The damage is evident from the holes they leave behind.

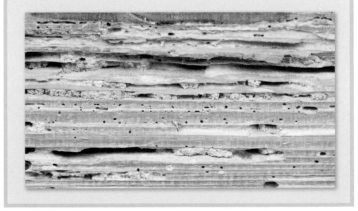

WHEN DO DRAGONFLIES EAT?

Dragonflies are impressive insects with two pairs of powerful clear wings that enable them to catch insects on the wing. They have large eyes for spotting their prey. Dragonfly nymphs live in water and so the adults are usually seen near ponds, rivers and lakes. Some species have a feeding territory, which they guard from other dragonflies – their clattering wings can sometimes be heard as they battle. When they mate, most species fly around in tandem before they lay their eggs in the water or among the waterside vegetation. Dragonfly nymphs are active carnivores. They feed on other insects, but can catch tadpoles or even small fish. On the underside of the head is a flap called the mask. This is armed with sharp jaws and fangs. At rest it is folded, but it can shoot out to catch its prey.

Male emperor dragonfly

Broad-bodied Libellula

A DRAGONFLY CAN FLY AS FAST AS 48KM/H (32MPH)

FACT FILE

A dragonfly's eyes are large and give it almost all-around vision. They are sensitive to the slightest movement around them. If you look closely you will be able to see the individual facets of the eye. Each one contains its own lens; together they help form the image seen.

WHEN DO WATER-DWELLING INSECTS BREATHE?

Water bugs are found in all sorts of different types of freshwater habitats. They all breathe air and have to return to the surface of the water from time to time. Ponds and lakes are the best habitats for water bugs. Only a few species live in streams and rivers, except where the current is slow-flowing.

Adult water beetles have to breathe air. They do not have gills. Many have a supply of air beneath their wing cases or under the body, which they renew from time to time. Watch a beetle in a tank. Some species come to the surface tail-first, while others come to the surface head first. Count the number of times a beetle will visit the surface in an hour.

DID YOU KNOW THAT WATER BEETLES CAN FLY? IT'S TRUE — THEY DO SO WHEN THEY ARE LOOKING FOR SOURCES OF WATER TO INHABIT.

FACT FILE

Place a needle on a piece of paper in some water. As the paper sinks, the needle floats, showing surface tension. This same process allows the water boatman to 'walk' on water. It uses its legs like oars to swim.

WHY ARE SOME INSECTS BRIGHTLY COLOURED?

Chinese tiger beetle

Harlequin beetle

There are many different ways in which insects will try to protect themselves from their enemies. Some insects, such as wasps and ants, have powerful stings or are able to shower their attackers with poisonous fluid. The hoverfly does not sting, but its colouring is so like that of a wasp or bee that enemies are very wary of it. Other insects, such as stick insects, use camouflage. They look like the leaves and twigs among which they feed. The bright colouring on some insects warns its enemies that it may be poisonous.

• FACT FILE •

A ladybird is brightly coloured. It is a very useful insect in the garden as it will eat the aphids that eat plants and flowers.

HOW DOES A CATERPILLAR BECOME A BUTTERFLY?

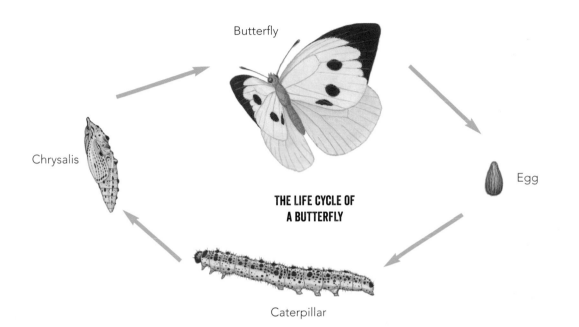

Butterfly

Chrysalis

THE LIFE CYCLE OF A BUTTERFLY

Egg

Caterpillar

During her lifetime a female butterfly can lay from one hundred to several thousand eggs. She is very careful to lay these eggs near the kind of plant that will be useful to her offspring later.

These eggs will hatch into tiny, wormlike grubs called 'caterpillar larvae' which begin to feed and grow immediately. They will shed their skins several times.

When the caterpillar feels it is time for a change, it spins a little button of silk to which it clings. It lands head down and sheds its caterpillar skin. It then appears as a pupa or chrysalis.

The pupa or chrysalis may sleep for some weeks or months. During this time it is undergoing a change, so that when it emerges from its chrysalid skin, it is a butterfly. It will spread its wings so that they can dry and become firm before it will attempt to fly.

• FACT FILE •

This hoverfly mimics a wasp, though it has no sting. It is an excellent flyer and can hover or fly backwacks or sideways if necessary. It feeds on nectar.

WHY DO MOTHS EAT WOOL?

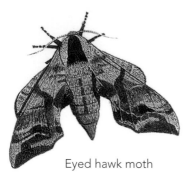

Eyed hawk moth

Death's head
hawk moth

Poplar hawk moth

There is a moth known as 'the clothes moth' and most people blame it for making moth holes in our clothes. But it isn't the moth that does the damage at all. The moth never eats; it lives only to produce its eggs and then it dies. It is when the young moth is in the caterpillar stage that all the damage is done.

The moth lays its eggs on woollen fabrics and, in about one week, the eggs hatch into caterpillars. The caterpillar then makes a little tubular case out of the wool, and lines this case with silk. There it lives as a caterpillar until it is ready to emerge as a moth. So you see that the problem of protecting clothes against moths is to make sure that moths have no chance of laying eggs on clothes.

• FACT FILE •

When at rest, an eyed hawk moth resembles a dead leaf. If alarmed, it opens its forewings to reveal striking eye markings on the hind wings. This is likely to scare predators such as birds.

WHAT IS A WASP'S NEST MADE OF?

There are two broad groups of wasps – social and solitary. The familiar yellow-and-black stripy wasps belong to the former group and live in colonies that may reach populations of 60,000 by the end of the summer.

In the spring, a queen wasp, on waking from winter hibernation, will start a new nest. Some species build nests in trees, while others prefer a small animal burrow in the ground. The queen will build a few cells, lay a few eggs to provide herself with workers and put paralyzed insects into the cells for the grubs to feed on as they grow. Once hatched, they will take over the work of building cells and finding food.

The cells are made of a form of paper: the wasps chew wood and mix it with saliva to make hexagonal cells. Unlike cells in honeycomb, cells in wasps' nests are arranged in rings and point down.

Solitary wasps lay a few eggs in cells in a hole in the ground and provide food. They have no workers.

HOW DOES A CRICKET PRODUCE ITS SONG?

Crickets are well known for their songs. These songs are produced primarily by the males. Each kind of cricket has a different song, usually trills or a series of chirps. Crickets produce sound by rubbing their two front wings together. They hear sound with organs in their front legs. Their songs help male and female crickets find each other. Male tree crickets sing in chorus. Their song is a high-pitched treet-treet-treet.

A cricket is a type of jumping insect related to the grasshopper. Crickets differ from grasshoppers in several ways. The wings of most crickets lie flat over each other on top of their backs. Other crickets only have tiny wings or are wingless. The slender antennae are much longer than the body in most kinds of cricket. Crickets are commonly found in pastures, meadows and along roads. Sometimes they even enter houses. These insects eat plants and the remains of other insects. The best-known are the house cricket of Europe and the common cricket of the United States.

Cricket

Grasshopper

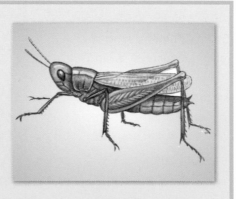

HOW ARE PLAGUES OF LOCUSTS FORMED?

A SWARM OF 50 MILLION LOCUSTS MIGHT EAT AS MUCH AS 423 MILLION POUNDS (192 MILLION KILOGRAMS) OF PLANTS EVERY DAY!

For thousands of years locust swarms have devastated farmland throughout Asia and Africa. A swarm can be as large as 50km (30 miles) long and contain more than 100,000 million locusts. A swarm of locusts can turn the sky totally black and wreak terrible damage on farmers' crops.

A locust is in fact a large grasshopper that normally lives a solitary and harmless existence. When their population builds up to a high level they begin to mass together and migrate in search of food. These migrations can cover many thousands of kilometres.

• FACT FILE •

Some animals pack themselves close together and move in unison as a herd. This makes it difficult for a predator to catch an individual animal.

WHAT ARE ARMY ANTS?

Army ants are fierce hunters. Most species travel across the land in narrow columns, while others hunt underground, moving through tunnels in the soil. Army ants prey chiefly on other insects and spiders. In some cases, they also kill and eat larger animals that cannot escape.

Army ants that live above ground do not build permanent nests. When they rest, they cling together in a large cluster. They may hang from the branch of a tree or roost inside a hollow log or other suitable place. The queen and her brood nest within the large cluster of bodies.

Some kinds of army ant hunt for a few weeks and then rest for a few weeks. During the hunting periods, they may nest at a different site every night. During the resting periods, they stay in one place, and the queen lays hundreds or thousands of eggs.

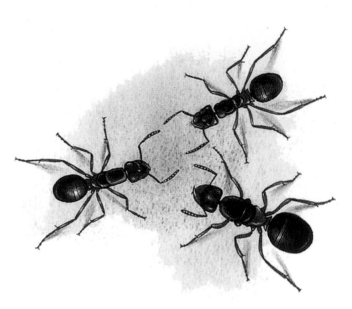

Most army ant colonies have between 10,000 to several million members.

FACT FILE

The black ant has a special relationship with aphids. They collect the sweet honeydew from the aphids and in return protect them from predators such as ladybirds.

WHY DO MOSQUITO BITES ITCH?

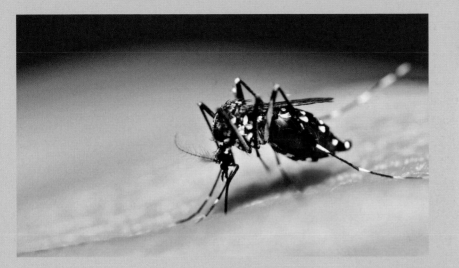

Only female mosquitoes bite and only the females of a few species attack human beings and animals. Mosquitoes do not really bite because they cannot open their jaws. When a mosquito 'bites' it stabs through the victim's skin with six needle-like parts called stylets which form the middle of the proboscis. The stylets are covered and protected by the insect's lower lip, called the labium.

As the stylets enter the skin, the labium bends and slides upwards out of the way. Then saliva flows into the wound through channels formed by the stylets. The mosquito can easily sip the blood because the saliva keeps it from clotting. Most people are allergic to the saliva, and an itchy welt called a 'mosquito bite' forms on the skin.

• FACT FILE •

A mosquito is an insect that spreads some of the most serious diseases to people and animals. Some mosquitoes carry the germs that cause such deadly diseases as encephalitis, malaria, filariasis and yellow fever.

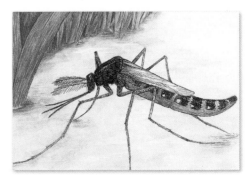

PICTURE CREDITS

Images supplied by Dreamstime

icons: Earth (5, 6–31) Fourleaflover; Sun (5, 32–57), Leaf (5, 58–91) Roberto Giovannini; Paws (5, 92–119) Jy26; Bird (5, 120–141) Sergey Yakovlev; Seahorse (5, 142–157) Sergey Markov; Moth (5, 158–175) Alexander Ryabintsev; Hand (throughout) Selman Amer.

8b Paul Piedra; 10b Maurie Hill; 11t Michal Bednarek; 11b Paul Banton; 12b Summersea; 13b Rfischia; 14t, 110b Outdoorsman; 14b Sergey Uryadnikov; 15b John.59; 16t Paul Prescott; 16b Erik Van Den Elsen; 17b Alisher Duasbaew; 20t Soundsnaps; 20b Sergei Butorin; 21t Gary718; 1b Elisa Bistocchi; 22t Adam Gryko; 22b Elena Elisseeva; 23l Stormboy; 23r Fabrizio Cianella; 24t Marco Regalia; 24b Martha Marks; 25l Valentin Armianu; 26b Jbphotographylt; 27b Igor Golovniov; 28t Youssouf Cader; 28b Niagaragirl; 29t Rolffimages; 29b Artisticco Llc; 30b Makhnach; 31t Chaoss; 31b Markus Gann; 34tl, 34tr Ashestosky; 34b Leo Bruce Hempell; 35b Shaye Beauford; 36b Vanessa Gifford; 37b Draghicich; 38b Iakov Kalinin; 39t Homydesign; 39b Roman Nedoshkovskiy; 40t Anthony Aneese Totah Jr; 41tl Wisconsinart; 41tr Jarvis Gray; 41b Oriontrail; 42b Brian Flaigmore; 43b Jesús Eloy Ramos Lara; 44b Martine De Graaf; 45t, 129t Satori13; 45b Nivi; 46t Joerg Habermeier; 46b, 119b Dirk Ercken; 47t Paweł Borówka; 47b Piboon Srimak; 49l Stephen Mcsweeny; 49r Andrew Grant; 51b Joerg Habermeier; 52t Erik Reis; 52b Digikhmer; 53t Smileus; 54t Rido; 55t Hsc; 56t Mzedig; 56b Mike Rogal; 57t Hungchungchih; 57b Dndavis; 60b Jonniewalker; 61l Kornwa; 62b, 68tl Carolina K. Smith M.d.; 63t Fantasista; 63b Eltoro69; 65b Felinda; 66t Inga Nielsen; 68c Yunxiang987; 68c Ignat Lednev; 69b Marsia16; 69r Luckynick; 70t Nike Sh; 72t, 134b Ben Goode; 72b Kts; 73t Clearvista; 74l Dirk Sigmund; 74r Lucadp; 75br Digoarpi; 76t Dean Pennala; 76b, 80t Czuber; 77br Jirkaejc; 78t Thomas Brandt; 78b Dave Winfield; 79t Dakfoto; 79bl Bruce Whittingham; 79br Pisotckii; 80b Naluphoto; 81br Jay O'brien; 82t Alain Lacroix; 82b Anton Foltin; 83br Raluca Tudor; 84t Swalters316; 84b Tan Kian Yong; 85b Derevianko; 86tl Natali572; 86c Motorolka; 86tr Ivandzyuba; 87b Joseph Gough; 90b Chris Moncrieff; 91t Ivan Mikhaylov; 94b Kutizoltan; 95t Lola Pidluskaya; 95b Boonyaruk Mung-on; 96cr Valentina Razumova; 96cl

Okea; 96b Dskow3; 97t, 116c Isselee; 98b Sergio Vila; 99b Rastislav Bado; 100t Chris Fourie; 100b Laschi; 101t Mike Rogal; 101b Wrangel; 102t Alain Lacroix; 102b Elshaneo; 103t Miroslav Beneda; 103b Geza Farkas; 104t Katarina Tilholm; 104b Indiansummer; 105t Dean Bertoncelj; 105b Alisbalb; 106t Miroslav Hlavko; 106b Martin Maritz; 107t Michal Bednarek; 108t Maria Itina, 108b Jakub Krechowicz; 109t Stefanie Van Der Vinden; 109b Debxan; 110t Lynn Bystrom; 111b 12qwerty; 112tl Lori Martin; 112tr Fabrizio Argonauta; 112b Shawn Jackson; 113t, 113b Cathy Keifer; 114t Bevanward; 114b Jayjaydy; 115t Vaughan Jessnitz; 115b Joel Santana; 116t John Kasawa; 116b Pius Lee; 117t, 131l Sam D\'cruz; 117b Mgkuijpers; 118b Alptraum; 122t Maksym Gorpenyuk; 122b Darren Baker; 123t Tom Dowd; 124l Wayne Duguay; 124r Mark Hryciw; 125t Maarten Van Der Kroft; 125b Geoffrey Kuchera; 126t Laryn Kragt Bakker; 126b Martingraf; 127b Connie Larsen; 128t Miketanct; 128b Zavgsg; 129b Marcel Rene Grossmann; 130b Gordon Miller; 131r Viter8; 132tl Michael Woodruff; 132tr Epstefanov; 132b Neil Burton; 133t Rory Daniel; 133c Subhash P.b; 134t Willtu; 135t Andrew Kerr; 135b Aurinko; 136t Stockthor; 136b Khunaspix; 137t Patrick Ager; 137b Bjfirestorm; 138t Oana Raluca Ghetu; 139t Dett; 139b Rikke68; 140b Catalinc; 141b Dsuman17; 144t Carol Buchanan; 144c Maceofoto; 144b Mietitore; 145b Mattiaath; 146t Hongqi Zhang (aka Michael Zhang); 147b Tan Raymond; 148t Sam Smith; 149b Jsphotography; 150b Brian Kushner; 151b Mikhail Blajenov; 152t Tim Heusinger Von Waldegge; 152b Melissaf84; 153t Pebat; 153b Jose Gil; 154b Clickamericas; 155t Lukas Blazek; 155b Wollertz; 156t Olga Khoroshunova; 156b Michael Herman; 157l Maria Dost; 157r Jocrebbin; 160b Serg_dibrova; 161t Shawn Zhang; 161b Piyathep; 162b Bildvision Bildvision Ab - Visby; 163b Irochka; 164t Sofiaworld; 164b Ermess; 165t Eerik Lehto; 165b Dalibor Duba; 167t Dmitry Zhukov; 168tl Shuyan Zhang; 168tr Mark Higgins; 169b Antti Siiskonen; 170b Ian Redding; 171b Thomas Lozinski; 173t Miguel Nicolaevsky; 174b Gordon Miller; 175t Mrfiza.

All other images copyright © Octopus Publishing Group Ltd